TRANSFORMATION AT THE SPEED OF PEOPLE

RICHARD W. BRIDGES

FriesenPress

Suite 300 - 990 Fort St
Victoria, BC, V8V 3K2
Canada

www.friesenpress.com

Additional contributors:
Andrew Ah Yong - Editor
Erin Pankratz - Editor
Farzaan Kassam - Editor
Joanne Campbell - Editor
Peggy Ah Yong - Editor

ISBN
978-1-03-911093-9 (Hardcover)
978-1-03-911092-2 (Paperback)
978-1-03-911094-6 (eBook)

1. BUSINESS & ECONOMICS, STRATEGIC PLANNING

Distributed to the trade by The Ingram Book Company

TABLE OF CONTENTS

For Rick,
loving father, husband, brother-in-law, uncle, mentor, coach and dear friend to
many....who left us far too soon.

Thank you Joanne, Farzaan, Erin, Peggy and Andrew.

An extraordinary team of dear friends, whose dedication and labour of love,
has brought Rick's dream to life.

FORWARD

The first time I met Rick Bridges is vividly etched into my memory. The lead up to that meeting had built to a crescendo of expectation; I was about to meet one of the greats, a future legend, and someone that my mentor, Joanne Campbell, co-editor of this book and someone who I admire greatly, had spoken so highly of.

When confronted with the reality of finally meeting Rick, I came away rather unimpressed. I recall sharing my first interaction with Joanne, much to her amusement; I got the impression that this wasn't the first time a person underestimated Rick. I just didn't see in him what Joanne did, but I decided to give it a shot and agreed to work side by side with Rick.

I can unequivocally say that my career trajectory to the C-Suite wouldn't have been possible without the knowledge that Rick shared. A number of our original "Quick Win" team members that Rick put together and trained have followed similar trajectories into great things, including taking senior roles at world-class transformative companies across industries spanning technology, finance, healthcare, telecommunications, real estate and consulting.

Rick was a unique mix of contradictions: unassuming while being blunt; content to be in the background, while, in reality being in control of the room; constantly joking, while at the same time, being laser-focused on finding solutions to very complex and serious problems. He had this overt simplicity that cloaked the complexity of his mind.

I left that first meeting thinking that I had nothing to learn from Rick and certainly nothing to fear; I couldn't have been more wrong. This was the genius of Rick; he was so unassuming that he completely freed you intellectually and mentally. He created an environment where you could learn, grow, and take risks, without fear of being humiliated.

Because Rick conveyed to people that he was the least smart person in the room, people felt comfortable to share their "dumb" ideas around him; many of these actually turned out to be pivotal and transformative ideas from frontline team members, the very layer that many companies systemically ignore.

Over a span of nearly a decade working together, we came to the realization that Rick held the keys to successful business transformation; with so many companies and people failing at transformation projects, we encouraged him to write a book so that more people and companies could benefit from his knowledge. The ideas that Rick shared with us in 2001 are just as relevant today, and I'm confident will be relevant for decades to come.

We were so fortunate to have had the opportunity to learn from Rick, and I hope that this book will help you to understand that you have the power to transform the world around you, regardless of whether you are a frontline worker or a CEO. The next time you meet someone and walk away unimpressed, you may want to recall the greatest lesson Rick taught me, that there is knowledge and wisdom in every human being, just waiting to be unleashed.

As you read this book, I ask that you picture a humble Rick speaking to you, imparting his knowledge with wry humour and quick wit. No question you ask will be ridiculed, and no idea too extreme to be considered. It's through this lens that I believe you will capture the most from this book.

Good luck on your transformation journey!

Farzaan Kassam

INTRODUCING MYSELF

Who am I to write this book?

I have no degrees, I'm not an industry leading expert, and I wouldn't even consider myself as someone with a successful career climbing the corporate ladder. But in the 30 years of my corporate career in telecommunications, energy and healthcare, I've been the victim, the willing agent, and creator (or the perpetrator, if you will), of transformation project failures that companies experience on a regular basis.

Because my career was so unspectacular, I didn't have a lot to lose, so when the opportunity to transform a customer organization arose years ago, it afforded me the chance to risk and try something different. I was able to take a different and somewhat counter intuitive approach to implementing technological change in a real business environment that was, and still is, very successful.

My approach to transformation is threefold:

1. **Value add:** Transformation provides a minimum return on your investment of 400% with real tangible results.

2. **Inconspicuous:** Transformation successfully implements enterprise-wide processes and systems without any hoopla or fanfare, to the point where it's considered a happy accident.

3. **Intuitive:** Transformation is so simple, so easy to replicate that it's considered in equals parts, common sense, luck, "sleight of hand" and wizardry.

Over the course of this book I'll chronicle in detail three "Bridges Principles", rules of implementation that guide change, explain how they work, show how to structure them as a real working business program, and put in place the necessary connections and interfaces for synchronizing with the goals, strategies and aspirations of a company.

Applied correctly, these principles will give your company a bridge to move from the past to the future, while realizing tangible benefits today, enhancing the vision of tomorrow and creating willing profitable partners in change, instead of vengeful, seemingly obedient victims. They will help you create a robust plan for creating a simple organization that does straightforward things devoted to the recovery and regeneration of a company's bedrock in preparation for change.

These principles have evolved from a real-world, working experiment I started in a leading national telecommunications provider. This program is still active and generating tens of millions of dollars in audited annualized benefit and hundreds of millions of dollars in accumulated benefits and competitive advantage; in addition to the financial benefits, this organization has also received external, international recognition for its superior execution of transformative programs.

These concepts are not proprietary but based upon the collective public knowledge gathered in many seemingly disparate fields like civil engineering, psychology, philosophy, economics, anthropology, and computer science. Through trial and error, these concepts have been brought together and honed into a structured approach to help implement change at low cost and successfully, in the real, working business environment.

During my time creating and nurturing what I call my Quick Win Collaboration Team, my own team, people in the company and even those inside the organization totally misunderstood what this transformation effort was about. Some people believed our accomplishments were achieved through magic, while others thought we were somehow pulling the wool over people's eyes. Those close to the experiment thought it was a new form of recruitment and a leadership development program, most saw it as a quick and dirty "skunkworks" shop to build software applications, and the remaining saw it as a pool of cheap labour to borrow from for whatever flight of fancy they may have.

I became too busily immersed in the daily work of propelling this transformation effort forward to explain it in any way or fashion that others may have hoped to understand; to be candid, I didn't fully appreciate all the newly uncovered aspects of this experiment as it was happening. That's why I had to stop, leave the daily grind of corporate life, sit down, and write this book.

INTRODUCING THE PROBLEM

I've been gravely concerned for some time about an epidemic sweeping the business world, a chronic dumbing-down disorder that's similar to Alzheimer's. Now this may appear to be a ludicrous statement as corporations are not like real people – they can't get diseases, can they? If you take into account the avalanche of technological advances, innovation and ingenuity pouring into our everyday work environment, it seems silly to suggest that somehow our companies are not as smart as they once were, and yet that's exactly what I'm suggesting.

Companies are sparing no expense using new things, trying new ways and building mountains of data, information and knowledge while doing it. However, those mountains don't necessarily bring opportunity, advantage or success because they are often lacking the strong foundation needed to build substantive value, that stable bedrock of tried and true corporate wisdom or legacy, which I call the working intellectual capital of corporations. It's a foundation built on the firm grasp of the present that connects both the important things done in the past with the important things we hope to do.

THE PROBLEM

Without this bedrock of intellectual capital, we end up in a disconnected state stuck between who we are and who we wish to become, with no understanding of how to get there. The effects of that disconnectedness can often be heard or felt in the boardrooms, books, blogs, tweets, and coffee shops all around the world. Consider these examples of corporate disconnectedness:

- **Inconsistent messaging:** Executives simultaneously talk about getting back to core values while also needing to transform the business.

- **Contradicting strategies:** Managers pursue pennies of operational efficiency with pounds of hopefully innovative ideas.

- **Wishful pursuit of simplicity:** CIO's and architects trying to return to the simpler past of one system, one vendor, or one standard, while at the same time introducing more evolving and complex forms of technology while doing it.

Just like Grandma and her senior moments, the disorientation of losing grasp with the present causes important projects to wander aimlessly, leaders to repeat the same mistakes while thinking they're trying something new, and companies to pay double the price to buy something they already own. Companies are spending too much on trying to implement change whether enabled by IT, process or organizational change. The cost to companies in lost money and productivity is obscene. The cost in human capital and lost knowledge is staggering.

Here is a cynical joke told in many a large company's hallways:

> *How does a CIO double their life span? The answer: The CIO enters into a co-sourcing partnership with a consulting firm, fires them after two years for not delivering, and then takes another two years to try it themselves.*

Of course, it's not all the consultant's fault. In an effort to stem chronic disappointment and complaints from businesses, a great deal of ingenuity has been brought to bear by technology vendors and purveyors of business process/improvement in order to advance the functionality, design, testing and implementation of these long sought-after transformational solutions.

Decades of effort, however, failed to solve the chronic disappointment and that's why more recently the focus has shifted on our approaches to change management, user acceptance, and what seems to be the burgeoning new science of project management, complete with its ability to manage expectations and commit to ruthless execution in ever-increasing incremental steps. All of these efforts have done some good; things that have helped to improve or fix some of the issues, but at the end of the day, much like masked surgeons confident in their own preparations and an operating room full of machines that go ping, **corporations must stop before making that first incision and ask one very important question, "Is the patient ready for the operation?"**

When the average person walking the halls of most companies happens to hear that the executive team is launching a project for "change", the first gut reaction is a tightening of the bowels as they know this is going to be a money-losing, time- sucking and often, career-ending proposition. Hence the need to resist instead of embrace change, however futile the attempt, in the hopes of avoiding the extraordinary upset and cost that's to follow. Now a great many people may argue that successful change is the life-blood of business today and that our Internet, TVs, and magazines are full of shining examples of profitable change. However, any person who has worked for any length of time can acknowledge that for every publicized happy accident, there are at least nine examples of expensively planned failed attempts that have been, if not fully, then partially, swept under the rug by creatively amortizing the benefits into the distant millenniums, or hiding the true financial impacts by robbing from every department budget to the point of almost certain mutiny, leaving most managers and employees with a gut wrenching connection to the saying "Giving until it hurts". So, it's in this environment that our initial intuitive reactions hardly make fertile fields for the seeds of successful change.

For my money, too much attention has been focused on the success and failure of the end-state target and end-state solutions brought on by the desired transformation. Usually no amount of money, recognition or coercion is spared when it comes to introducing or indoctrinating everybody in the company to the new end-state and their new supporting solutions, whether everyone or everything is ready or not. Yet if you've sat through enough post-mortem reviews on failed corporate transformation exercises, typically the first 25 percent of the slide presentation is devoted to how the lack of employee engagement, the lack of executive support, the high project churn rate of key personnel and the changing business requirements were at the heart of the failure. The remaining 75 percent of the presentation is devoted to the rescue plan for that investment, the great opportunities still available, the great things that were learned, and what not to do next time. Of course, if there is a next time, everyone involved this time will make darn sure they're as far away as humanly possible.

So here's the thing, the real corporate value in change always lies in the journey being taken. However, too often the journey is short-changed, short-circuited, and limited to a select few. Why? Because of the astronomically expensive burn rates that approach tens, even hundreds, of thousands of dollars daily, needed to maintain momentum for huge corporate transformation projects and their solutions.

We're failing all across the world at a prodigious rate and company reputations are at stake, so we've collectively lowered our expectations and aspirations, while at the same time raising the amount of money spent in an attempt to guarantee success. It has gotten to the point where executives seriously try to rationalize spending hundreds of millions of dollars as "mission accomplished" while dealing with half-finished pieces of technology, too often added to an already complex mishmash of legacy systems and a new but rudimentary web front end. All of this requires some out-sourced center of cheap labour to manually work in the background locating and processing lost transactions caused by those "successfully implemented" project pieces.

To make matters worse, our senior moments are exacerbated by the time in which we live. Thanks to the computer chip, bandwidth, and unprecedented connectivity, we have a glut of data, information, and their close sibling, knowledge. This glut has been a relentless assault on the senses of both people and companies to the point that all of our time is devoted to filtering things, and not about openly inviting the sensing, thinking about and trying new things in our current surroundings. Go into any office building, pick any company, become a fly on the wall of any meeting room in use at that moment, and you will start to see very clearly the results of that sensory overload and the rapid filtering tactics required to survive in such an environment. 90% of any meeting attendees must simultaneously sliver their attention span between the presenter, their smart phones, chat messages from the webinar session on their laptops, and the side conversations from their seat mates.

Access to information and knowledge has become such a commodity that we demand it be packaged in bite-size pieces complete with all the bona fides of authenticity and a concise summary that ensures efficient cataloguing into our brains so it can be called upon at a moment's notice without thought. If it does not come in that form, then that knowledge is met with misconception, rejection, or apathy.

Thanks to our mass production approaches to knowledge, the amount we are accessing in this age at any given moment is staggering, but the amount we are retaining and integrating into our environment is not. In fact, we are starting to know less and less about more and more until one day we will all know absolutely nothing about everything. This bedrock of the present corporate legacy was how companies in the past gained enough leverage for profit and advantage. In today's dynamic business environment, unless you're constantly reaffirming and rediscovering who you are, you're doomed to a living hell, wishing you could go back and incapable of seeing a way forward.

THE PROBLEM IN ACTION

It's clear to me that we've forgotten some basic truths about wanting to change something for the better. When I'm out and about going to business conferences, walking on to a golf course and joining a threesome of strangers, or striking up a conversation with some parents I don't know on the sideline of a sport field or rink, I like to conduct a little test to see if things are getting any better out there in the business world by asking some very basic questions about their work. In short order, I usually start to hear one of three similar stories that illustrate how, even with the best of intentions, companies continually shoot themselves in the foot when aspiring to be better while frustrating their employees to no end. These stories are all symptomatic of the consequences of not differentiating the type of change being dealt with and preparing for opportunity prior to embarking on the journey for change. I call these stories:

1. **Shuffling the Deck Chairs**
   Reorganizations that are designed in the misguided hope that business culture can be passed on or reinforced by changing the inanimate organizational structure.

2. **Flavour of the Month Club**
   Each new leader brings a mandate to shift the business, but repetitive cycling of cultural mandates and leaders deepens the cynicism of workers and creates an embedded resistance to change.

3. **Premature Transformation**
   An example of a self-inflicted chronic performance anxiety disorder which causes corporate desires to get ahead of corporate reality, and project plans to get ahead of what's possible to deliver.

The examples of failure are well chronicled, and I need not spend time giving them here. If you're someone involved in the corporate world today, you have many of your own personal horror stories to prove what I've written as true. My belief is that it does not have to be this way. By understanding the underpinnings of change, we can learn from ourselves and others and revisit how to transform our company.

THE SOLUTION – THE BRIDGES PRINCIPLES

My approach is based upon three simple principles:

1. **You need to change not knowing into knowing.**
   Thanks to the pace of business today and the growing complexity of technology all around us, we're no longer experts in anything. Business today requires a structured operational approach at rediscovering that which used to be known and is being lost daily. This rediscovered knowledge in the context of current and future business conditions leads to a better understanding of what changes are possible, probable, and plausible.

2. **Managing your knowledge like an asset is essential for transformation success.**
   Where we decide and plan to start change in our companies is usually dictated by external needs and without understanding of the internal readiness and capability in those areas. It's our business knowledge and how it's leveraged in that business area that's the foundation for successful change. We need to prepare that knowledge so it can support and enhance the desired changes. This requires us to look at our intellectual capital in a different way that allows us to convert it into the right forms for automation, process optimization, new roles, new partnerships or relationships and new business units.

3. **Successful transformation requires preparing the site for change.**
   Our management practices, the way we organize our companies, and the value we assign to certain skills and roles, actually hold back change, or even entrench behaviours that resist the very changes we're trying to implement. So, we need to understand these necessary forces that keep the corporate structure intact and how to counteract them, for a moment in time, precisely in the areas we need to invite or tempt actions for change.

When it comes to transformation and making change happen, companies no longer have the luxury or appetite to be throwing around large sums of money and resources trying to affect change. The term "transformation" has become a dirty word to describe the expensive process of bulldozing change. The world continues to become more complex, leaving us with a great sense of inadequacy when it comes to expertly leading sustainable and effective corporate change. Paying astronomical sums of money on the best experts to help guide, plan, and execute change feels like the right thing to do, but still tends to bring less than spectacular results.

If you take the time to investigate the smash hits in management best practices and where they originated, you start to see a clear pattern. So, what would happen if you started the journey for change today before you know what to change, and did it daily but for dollars a day?

> *How much better would your goals, designs, and plans be?*
> *How much better prepared and engaged would the company,*
> *the leadership, and the employees be?*
> *How much cheaper and quicker would transformation be if*
> *you put the learning ahead of the big money spent?*

BRIDGES PRINCIPLE 1: CHANGE NOT KNOWING INTO KNOWING

SHUFFLING THE DECK CHAIRS

Our first story is "Shuffling the Deck Chairs", which is about reorganizations that are designed in the cyclonic misguided hope that the collection of common positive human attributes and values we call business culture like "customer first", "do it right the first time", and "service with a smile" can be passed on or reinforced by changing the inanimate organizational structure. That song has been played repeatedly. Want to be leaner and quicker? Then go with a horizontal structure. Want to maximize profit and quality? Then go with a vertical structure. Want more visibility and control? Then centralize. And on and on we go.

If you stop to think about it, there's great precedent here that justifies this type of action. When you're buying clothes, if you want to look slimmer you wear black, if you want to look taller you wear vertical stripes, if you want to run faster you put on those fancy running tights. But the fact remains you're not slimmer, taller, or faster because of it. Reorganizations give the reassuring appearance of change and we hope that by shuffling the deck chairs, we can break complacency, force people to reassess their competencies and embrace the new mantras, be it cheaper, better, faster or whatever human quality it's being aspired to.

There's an old and great truth in an old fable about the ass and the old shepherd that changing masters does not change the work.

A Shepherd, watching his Ass feeding in a meadow, was alarmed all of a sudden by the cries of the enemy. He appealed to the Ass to fly with him, lest they should both be captured, but the animal lazily replied, "Why should I, pray? Do you think it likely the conqueror will place on me two sets of panniers?" "No," rejoined the Shepherd. "Then," said the Ass, "as long as I carry the panniers, what matters it to me whom I serve?".

Reorganizations are not the way to prepare for change; all they do is signal the start of that same old change, and they have two very debilitating impacts at a time when companies can least afford them. That undesired complacency which is the target of the reorganization, now becomes a very attentive and fortified resistance to change. It's an insipid form of resistance as it looks and feels like compliance but is actually intentional passive resistance. It will promote blind obedience to all that puts in peril the desired changes.

Secondly, instead of driving reflection on the core competencies or on the way things are done, the intellectual capital that's the life blood of that organization immediately leaves for greener pastures, or if it does remain, it's hidden and jealously guarded. This further entrenches the old ways of thinking; the new people coming in don't possess that same level of intellectual capital and will get outfitted with the same "two sets of panniers", and will in very short order start to exhibit all the same behaviours as those left behind.

The hopes and aspirations for that reorganization and the resulting cultural shift will die a slow death, so if you re-organize at the start, the best laid plans will fall apart, but if you re-organize at the end, you will get lots of help from your partners and friends. Also, you'll have saved the company about 15% in increased operating costs by avoiding all that confusion at a time when clarity and understanding is required.

If you want to create that cultural shift, then reorganize those "two sets of panniers" and the circumstances that put them there. This constant shuffling has created a chronic disease in 21st century businesses that I call "Corporate Alzheimer's", and avoiding aluminum pots won't help. This dumb-down brain-drain of a corporation's intellectual capital has mostly been hidden because companies or at least industries over the last 30 years, have been able to cycle that intellect around amongst itself.

Over the next 20 years that intellect, or more importantly the heads that contain that intellect, will be disappearing from the workforce and the cost to reacquire and codify that intellect will be beyond the capability of most businesses. That loss of intellect is very noticeable when you show up for those requirement meetings on critical parts of the business and are surrounded by junior people, people new to the company, and people with a vested interest in not changing.

The truth is, no matter how knowledgeable the new people are, they will never *know* as much as the intellect that has left. Information and knowledge are the cold, hard and impersonal facts that appear to stand on their own, can be moved, manipulated and measured with great certainty and great efficiency. Knowing, on the other hand, is much more time consuming to obtain and much more personal, as it builds a web of connections relating all that data and knowledge. It's gained by battle testing our perception of the facts in different situations, and thanks to those experiences, helps to define and prove the recurring and often pragmatic foundational working truth. Especially true today, thanks to the degree of variability in the business environment, it's a shrinking pool of this working wisdom that companies rely on to gain competitive advantage, drive value, and promote the promise of a brighter future.

The difference between knowledge and knowing is a very subtle one, but the results when one is applied over the other are dramatic. I would sometimes conduct a cheap experiment on that subtle difference between knowledge and wisdom during formal settings like a meeting or job interview. I would ask attendees, "What do you need to be a true leader?" and of course they usually rattled off the typical laundry list of attributes associated with good leaders. In short order I would meet those same people in an informal setting and after a chat, a laugh or a beer, would ask the same question and the answer was also in a fashion typical, as a wry little smile would unfold across their face when they answered, "why followers, of course!"

Such is the fine line between the facts of knowledge and connecting truth through knowing. Such is the distinction between knowing what to do and doing it. **More so now than at any other time, a company's advantage is its ability to step over that line and tap into the knowing.**

THE BROKEN BRIDGE

What is eroding knowing?

There are several factors both external and internal that are causing increased noise, distraction, and disorientation to the point they have eroded a company's ability to leverage the working end of knowing. Primary among them are:

- Technology

- Globalization

- Information Explosion

TECHNOLOGY

First, technology became more accessible and complicated, all at the same time. The actual footprint of technology used by even the smallest and most non-technical of industries has grown larger over the decades. This is true even if you forget about all the instrumentation and robotics associated with manufacturing and production, and focus only on the simplest aspects of business, taking orders, tracking invoices, managing the bookkeeping, and general communications. The footprint has grown from what used to be desks, filing cabinets and bookcases filled with books, ledgers, pencils, pens, and typewriters, to include terminals, mainframes, servers, networks, laptops, enterprise and desktop applications, wireless networks, wiki resources, web services, portals, and more.

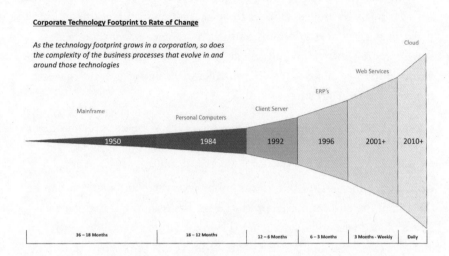

Corporate Technology Footprint to Rate of Change

As the technology footprint grows in a corporation, so does the complexity of the business processes that evolve in and around those technologies

Cloud

Web Services

ERP's

Mainframe

Client Server

Personal Computers

| 1950 | | 1984 | 1992 | 1996 | 2001+ | 2010+ |

| 36 – 18 Months | 18 – 12 Months | 12 – 6 Months | 6 – 3 Months | 3 Months - Weekly | Daily |

Like counting the rings on a tree, you can tell how old a company is by the different layers of technology that never go away, regardless of age, only to be buried by a newer layer. Soon the foundation of ever newer and more complicated technology is resting on the assumptions made of long forgotten and unseen layers of logic. There's great knowledge of the different layers and what they are. But no one knows how they relate and work together.

GLOBALIZATION

Next is globalization, which is a perfect illustration for the "butterfly effect" – that often talked about concept that of a small thing having a potentially profound impact on a complex system. So, as a butterfly in the rain forest of Malaysia could flap its wings and cause a tornado in Oklahoma, in business it's an executive in Singapore who flaps his gums and causes a customer to close their account, ruining that executive's company. They in turn default on their loan, which is the tipping point that causes an investigation into some banker's affairs. That investigation uncovers massive fraud, causing a British bank to collapse, which other financial institutions are heavily vested in. This causes financial institutions in the United States to tighten credit, choking off the much needed cash for many businesses all over the place, which increases unemployment, causing people to default on their mortgages, sub-prime or not, driving more banks to go belly up and so on and so forth, until the entire world economy collapses. You get the picture; it makes everything seem haphazard and arbitrary.

Closer to home and more obvious to employees is the example of one of Ford's automotive assembly plants in the US, which since the late '90s was recognized for being the most productive car factory on the continent. But in the early 2000s, it was announced the plant would run until the end of the current model product line. The reaction of the plant's union official was understandable: "I think it's a slap in the domestic market's face," the union official said, "They've got the best work force in the world here, they indicate they're going to stake the future on the work force, and then they give them the status quo and the new product goes to the Mexicans and Canadians." In the mid-2000s, the plant was closed and the property eventually sold so that a conference center, hotel, and parking lot could take its place. This is hardly news any more as people have come to expect it. But just because people have come to expect it doesn't mean this hasn't eroded the level of trust and increased the level of paranoia an employee has in their company, their boss, and their job.

External factors that cause budgetary belt-tightening that results in layoffs and "right-sizing", or worse, a total catastrophe as the company is forced to go belly up, makes job performance an arbitrary factor in maintaining employment. Having seen the most productive divisions, factories, offices or people get closed down, right-sized, or out-sourced because somewhere halfway around the world there's someone else with similar skills, at a cheaper wage, in an area that offers better tax breaks willing to do the job, proves that the days when you could count on joining a company and staying there for 30 years are gone. Heck, whole industries can come and go in less than half that time in today's business environment.

This has forced employees to become very portable expecting to move at least five times in their career, if not more. Smart people today must be career mercenaries and look at employment in much broader terms than just salary and stability. These mercenaries must take into consideration the position of the company in its industry and the prospects for both that company and the industry over the short term. Then they must look at the role of the job and gauge the weight of the experiences and development offered that will enhance that employee's resumé, making them that much more marketable.

This has created a higher rate of workforce churn than at any other time in the history of modern companies.

This relentless increase in workforce churn, decade after decade, has greatly eroded both the level of trust and the amount of tacit intellectual capital or knowing that's available to be leveraged by a company. This churn is pouring tacit intellectual capital out the door. What little bit that's left have employees driven by misgivings and paranoia hiding away what they know in the hopes of increasing protection and security.

I've often wondered, speaking as a baby boomer, if this sense of entitlement that has been so often associated with Generations X and later, is more so the natural outcome of living in this new reality, where investing in the collective good – when that collective is mercurial and unstable – is much less compelling than an investment that brings a return in a much more tangible and personal way.

INFORMATION EXPLOSION

Another impact has been the much talked about information explosion. One only has to look at something as simple as a birth certificate to appreciate just how much this information explosion has overrun our ability to know.

In the '80s, a hospital would collect approximately 280 bytes of information on that birth, today that number is closer to 2,000 bytes. An expert on birth certificates would have to collect eight times more information from that birth certificate than an expert in the '80s. The amount of time anyone has is finite, which means in order to maintain your level of expertise, you have to cut out a lot of other extracurricular activity and narrow your focus just so you can keep up. The paradox of this age of information is that the experts of the world have to know more about less until one day they will know absolutely everything about nothing. Thanks to that explosion of information, the concept of expertise is becoming extinct and along with it, our confidence in others and their ability to do the "right" things, and in ourselves, about knowing our jobs.

THE BROKEN BRIDGE BETWEEN KNOWLEDGE AND KNOWING

If we look back to the '50s and '60s, every company in just about every segment of business from avionics to waste management had an abundance of tenured employees with 30+ years of experience or employees aspiring to become like those tenured employees. Along with this came a somewhat stable business environment. Companies that were very siloed could draw on a high level of internal expertise for consistent evolving productivity. Add to that a limited array of technology used by that company and strategy/business planning cycles that averaged around five years in length, and you pretty much had a guaranteed recipe for creating a lot of knowing to go along with that knowledge to bridge to your future business goal.

What is markedly different back in those days was you had the time to mix things together, from the top down to create the assumptions, hypotheses, and theories, and have them vetted from the bottom up with many scenarios. People had time to synthesize the old with the new; to experiment, compromise, and modify. The typical change cycle in a company was 18 months for strategy & planning, 18 months for implementation, and two years for burn in. It was in this environment that the basic methodology for change used today was created and refined for software, process, or people.

Call it the "waterfall" method or not, it became a top-down flow of requirements gathering, designing, planning, implementing, verifying, and maintaining change. It worked fine, because most of the blanks got filled in before flowing onto the next step. Change was a bidirectional or alternating process that allowed you to get the answers to the critical questions that were going to be asked by involving that bottom-up vetting process.

So, what happened to change all this? External pressures forced companies to compress the average strategy cycle and the resulting bouts of change down to less than two years. This meant that strategy, planning and implementation have almost become parallel processes. As for burn-in time at the working level, that's now considered outside the scope of any project of change and is merely the time needed for the business to accept what has been delivered.

Change today is run mostly with the expectation that all will be accepted verbatim and where there are issues, that compromise will be the order of the day. The compression of this cycle has forced most of the time and energy to focus on accommodating the top down activities of strategy, planning, and implementation with the appropriate tools and approaches. Virtually no time has been spent figuring out how to streamline the bottom-up processes of vetting and acceptance for that change.

WHY WE NEED TO FIX THE BRIDGE

In the end, Alzheimer's-inducing factors including shorten change cycles with increased complexity, in addition to globalization and the information explosion, have eroded the level of confidence that we have in what we know. We get angry and paranoid when we don't get the time to understand. We wander aimlessly when we forget more than we remember. We rummage around for those things just outside our grasp and hide those things that are in them. We remain in an agitated and wakeful state, never sleeping as we're bombarded with more and more incomprehensible stimuli.

Memory loss, confusion, disorientation, and poor judgment are absolutely frightening symptoms when they're regularly exhibited in our parents or grandparents going through their senior moments. But in the business world we look at the chronic disconnections that cause important projects to wander aimlessly, groups of people to repeat the same mistakes over and over while thinking they're trying something new, and companies paying double to buy something they already own, as the price to be paid when dealing with change in today's complex world. Instead, these are real warning signs for an incessantly progressive disease that acts just like Alzheimer's and is eroding company's ability to know.

It's thought that Alzheimer's is brought on by a build-up of certain types of protein in the brain that interferes with communication between neurons caused by growths called plaques and tangles. Similarly, the information explosion, globalization, and our mass production approach to managing business are causing interference with the growth of a company's intellectual capital by eroding the confidence, acumen and the will needed to pull off change successfully. The growth of project management is the outcome of trying to manage the symptoms of this disease much in the same way a caregiver looks after an Alzheimer's patient.

When reading the most typical symptoms Alzheimer's caregivers must manage, and their remedies, it rings eerily familiar to wise and seasoned advice given to project managers when learning the art of managing their clients.

Before you start any journey for meaningful change or transformation, you must first repair the damage caused by this dementia of mistrust by rebuilding confidence through knowing, and the first person anyone must come to trust again, is themselves.

THE PARADOX OF CHANGE

Speak out loud the words *project failure* and you will instantly start a great debate about whether or not businesses are actually failing at change or transformation. This is a classic case of the "half-filled glass" scenario. The practitioners of change and by that I mean people involved in the planning, designing and delivery of change, will argue the case for the "glass being half full" based upon the improving results declared by seemingly scientific surveying, gleaned from various decade-long studies, or because of the successful proliferation of technology into every aspect of business and society. These facts are considered proof that the term *failure* is imprecise when it comes to the success rate of change and their associated projects. Meanwhile, the recipients of change, and by that I mean the people who are expected to be responsive, agile and pay for this change, offer a case for the "glass being half empty" as experience has taught them with morbid resignation that it's going to be a difficult, time consuming, and costly affair with a relatively low rate of return for such a high level of investment.

Looking back over the last three decades, this push-pull between whether the glass is half full or half empty has forced us into playing a blame game that has filled our Internet, books, magazines, and meeting rooms with frenzied passionate finger pointing. In terms of transformational projects, it's not uncommon to hear the sales folks blame the business operations and in turn the business operations blame IT. IT usually blames simultaneously the users and the vendors. The vendors usually blame other vendors or consultants and the customer blames whichever live body they can get a hold of.

Of course, it's not just vendors and consultants getting the brunt of the blame, but a great deal has been heaped on top of technology itself. Now a lot of effort and ingenuity has been brought to bear by many over the decades and it has not been in vain. We have seen both a good deal of advancement in the functionality and interoperability of the technology and refinement in the methods for designing, testing, and implementing these long sought-after transformational solutions. Despite the decades of effort, however, chronic disappointment is more often than not still the outcome. More recently, the focus on this improvement has shifted to our approaches on change management, user acceptance, and to what seems to be the burgeoning new science of project management, complete with its ability to manage expectations to the lowest common denominator and commit to ruthless execution in ever-increasingly smaller and irrelevant incremental steps.

So while I can't deny the facts supporting the belief that the glass is half full, on the other hand and thanks to one accidentally insightful moment, I was offered a clear view of why the perception of the glass being half empty is so very real. It came during a rather contentious meeting with my company's corporate comptroller some years back. In that meeting he was openly and rather passionately accusing me of "criminally padding the benefits" for one of the recently completed projects I was leading.

Now prior to my meeting with this corporate comptroller, he had just finished spending several weeks writing off that corporation's most recent "*successful*" implementation of transformational change and with impeccable timing, my little project gave him the first real chance for cathartic release from the sins of writing off that transformation, and also allowed him to renew his quest to never let it happen again. Over the next 60 minutes, he gave me a world-class pummeling and it was near the end of my beating that he spoke a set of words that struck me like a lightning bolt and summed up the reality of what is the true perceived corporate success rate for change. He said, "If I took all the estimated benefits used to justify the money this company has spent on transformation over the last 10 years, technically, we should have zero employees." At that time, the company had about 30,000 employees. It illustrated very eloquently the truth behind the dance that IT, business, and finance has been reduced to, in order to fund any type of successful change in most companies and it usually ends up being the type of change we must do while both simultaneously winking one eye, crossing our fingers behind our backs, and holding our collective noses.

So, what is the truth? Is the glass half empty or is it half full? Does it matter? The answer is, it does matter, because what is needed to make any change truly successful is a full glass.

THE MISSING HALF

The reason change is so darn difficult and expensive (regardless of whether you think it was a failure, challenge, or roaring success) is because we are not starting off with a full glass. A full glass of what, you may ask? Well, half the glass has been filled with a lot of knowledge, but what is needed and missing to make it a full glass is knowing. By knowing I mean the experiences that make up the bedrock of corporate wisdom, the confidence gained from having traveled familiar roads with familiar faces, that stuff used inside people's heads, those rules and routines buried deep inside our legacy systems and those key relationships that know and make decisions at critical points in our processes.

All the important insightful and innovative things learned from acting, achieving and doing the business are critical to any transformation. When I used to tell people the reason for our difficulties with change in business is because we don't know enough, I got either a look of incredulity followed by the stinging statement I'm an idiot, or a passionate litany of the efforts taken to ensure a project had all the empirical knowledge necessary to be successful.

Now these efforts to obtain knowledge were not insignificant. They include hiring the brightest experts money can buy, excessive diligence and detail in requirements gathering, expansive reviews of vendor products, exhaustive customer focus groups, and rigorous analysis of all the trending and survey data, but there is a difference between knowledge and knowing. It's the same difference that exists between being "book smart" and "street smart." All too often we spend all our time focused on the overt act of filling the glass with knowledge, in the hopes that it magically creates knowing.

In the end, regardless of how much knowledge is poured in, we only end up with half of what is needed. It's similar to someone with great knowledge that can explain in detail all aspects of a sport and yet they are unable to execute a single move. You know the old saying "Those that can't do, coach." The same thing holds true at the other end of the spectrum. Trying to fill that glass with a lot of knowing is still only half the equation for change. We see it all the time with certain athletes that know how to execute at an extremely high level of proficiency and yet are unable to articulate exactly how they do it. We enviously call these people intuitive, a natural, or gifted. They just go out and somehow do it. The question becomes, "Are they doing it the best they can?" Then there are the rest of us in between, not quite gifted, or not quite knowledgeable. Yet something miraculous happens when some of us put both knowledge and knowing together – we develop and grow.

The result may vary depending upon the starting point those individuals have with knowledge or knowing. But having command over both, regardless of what level, means you can change things, you can evolve, you can start to maximize the potential and maybe, just maybe, excel. The root of most problems with change attempted by companies is the simple act of placing too much emphasis on obtaining knowledge and not enough in knowing.

CAN KNOWLEDGE AND KNOWING WORK TOGETHER?

Knowledge and knowing comes out in radically different settings, even if that knowledge and knowing exists inside one person. Knowledge lives in the formal, knowing lives in the informal. Pour both into the same glass and they act like oil and vinegar, naturally separating into their own parts. It requires someone or something to continually mix the two together and bridge the settings, otherwise you just have a glass of oil and vinegar, instead of what should be the start of a really good salad dressing. To make sure your recipe for change or transformation isn't an accident waiting to happen, you need both ingredients, knowledge and knowing to form that solid foundation, and you need to consciously mix them together so the bedrock for that foundation sets and can support the change.

I got to see firsthand how focusing on just the top-down formal facts or knowledge of a situation without adding in the bottom up of what was known, can marginalize the truth of a situation, impede insight, and prevent success. In my first frontline management position as a supervisor for a team that programmed telephone lines, I was asked to join a task force to deal with service quality issues for our order process. The outside field people where chronically complaining that over 50% of the orders were incorrectly programmed, and traditionally my group, being the last ones to touch the orders before they were sent out to the field, usually took the brunt of that blame.

In preparation for the first meeting with the task force, I spent weeks pouring over all my metrics and to my surprise, we were meeting our target for order quality at 98%. When the task force got together, we reviewed the metrics for all seven teams involved in the process and found, much to everyone's surprise, that all of us were meeting our own order quality metrics at 98%.

So, while everyone was hoping for an obvious culprit and to point a finger at somebody, no one could. As a taskforce this posed quite a dilemma; we could not go back to the big bosses saying everything is fine and there's nothing to fix. Especially when there was ample loud and anecdotal evidence from the field that something was rotten.

So as a team we started to dive down into each other's business, taking a step-by-step look at how an order truly got created and then delivered. In a logical, systematic, measured fashion, we identified ten points of possible failure across the end-to-end process, and all points resided inside the seven teams involved within the task force. Next, we started to hand-measure the order quality at each of those points and found that the success rate was at 98% or better; considering this was a mature order process that had been refined over many years, the fact it worked with relative efficiency and consistency shouldn't have been unexpected. But this was a serial process, so if you multiplied 98% by 98% you get something less than 98%. Now do this ten times in a row and you get 82%, which is the optimum success rate you could expect from that process.

It was great we found the problem; it wasn't quite as bad as the field people were making it out to be, but it was below the overall end-to-end performance target for that process at 90%. We started to invest more time and energy into tweaking the process, eliminating some steps, improving quality standards at a few key points, and bada bing, bada boom, problem solved! Or so we thought. The cold, hard facts of two months' worth of verified metrics proved beyond a shadow of a doubt that now, as individual teams and as an overall process, we were meeting or exceeding all performance targets. We could show from an end-to end process perspective that 92% of all orders were being delivered correctly to the field.

Unfortunately, the feedback from the outside was "nothing had improved and in some cases that things had gotten so much worse, the clients had given up worrying about it. Our reaction was one of incredulity! Confident in the knowledge we had collectively gained, the veracity of our facts, the methodology used, the effort expended, and due diligence taken to get there, we immediately discounted this feedback as exaggerated and went about presenting our findings in great detail. Included in this presentation was an astronomical price tag to improve the process beyond the current 92%, just in case anyone including the big bosses still considered this to be a priority. We did a great job of proving our case, and the taskforce was disbanded along with many thanks and the requisite letters of commendation for the improvements we brought.

It wasn't until sometime later when I had realized that the root of the problem wasn't the process itself, or even what seemed like the exaggerated claims of error from the field. It was the common conventions used to make a company work, the unwritten rules if you will, that are used to accommodate groups of people, teams, and organizations so they can partner together for common purpose. If we as a taskforce had only tried to live in the reality of where the problem resided, and tried to understand the perceptions that persisted with the same effort we did the facts, maybe we could have been able to uncover what was unspoken or unwritten.

Armed with our knowledge and what was known, we could have lined both up and maybe caught a glimpse of something that was at the same time obscure and also very obvious. Every time I think back to my participation on that taskforce and how we overlooked the obvious, it reminds me of a poster I saw in a manager's office once. On it was the picture of several hands clasping one on top of the other. The caption below read, "MEETINGS – None of us are as dumb as all of us".

In this case what was overlooked was the metric itself. When a metric is tied to people's wages and bonuses, there's usually a great deal of work done to ensure that a set of criteria is put in place so the metric is fair and equitable for everyone involved. The last thing anyone wants, especially if it impacts your bonus, is allowing your downstream partner involved in that process, the ability to ding your metric with their sins. It just isn't sporting, and in this case the metric for delivered order quality had just such a criteria.

Of course these criteria were hammered out way back when the process was in its infancy and were not written or recorded anywhere except deep inside the hieroglyphic code of some long-lost programming language like COBOL or FORTRAN that ran the metrics on the old mainframe system. Now if my downstream partner doesn't deliver the work in the agreed upon timeframe, with all the agreed upon criteria, then all bets are off, and this order becomes an exception and isn't "measured".

What was known to those outside in the field was that more than 50% of orders are wrong. What was fact and recorded knowledge was that 92% of the orders are done correctly. The truth was that more than 50% of all orders including exceptions were wrong, and that 92% of the orders that qualified to be measured were done correctly. The insight was no one was really looking at exceptions and there was no adequate process to handle them.

Now this is a very simplistic example, and typically these unwritten conventions or rules that get in our way, are increasingly more complex, less obvious, and much more prevalent than we think.

Knowledge is an important top-down driven ingredient in the recipe for change, which flows from a verified source to a target, and from an expert to an implementer. **Knowing is just as important but is bottom-up driven,** pushing need into understanding and turning a novice to a wise veteran. Having both ingredients available provides the opportunity to gain insight and ideas. But mixing them together is what creates experiences that stimulate action, advantage and tangible value.

In the past, that full glass of knowledge and knowing has been something readily available in every company. Because these two ingredients were abundant, and the speed of change was such that action was a naturally occurring experience, then all conscious thought of this process was relegated to the periphery and taken for granted.

Ironically we now live in an age that offers companies an exponentially expanding buffet of knowledge, thanks to the microchip, connectivity, and bandwidth, while at the same time an information explosion, globalization, and our mass production approaches to managing business are eating away at a company's ability to know. This inability to know is creating an unhealthy imbalance between knowledge and knowing. This imbalance is slowly diminishing the weight of a company's intellectual capital, just like a compulsive eater that shovels in plate after plate of food, only to expunge it quickly before having a chance to digest it and gain the nutritional or caloric benefits from eating. Such an imbalance is no longer on the periphery of conscious thought in the scientific community and companies today are knowing less and less, about more and more. To recover, companies need to first stop the erosion of knowing going on in their company and then they need to worry about bridging the right experiences that promote action, advantage, and tangible value.

BRIDGES PRINCIPLE 2: MANAGING YOUR KNOWLEDGE LIKE AN ASSET

FLAVOUR OF THE MONTH CLUB

The second story is called "The Flavour of the Month Club" and it starts with a new leader being appointed with a mandate to shift the business. In a fit of unbridled commitment or genuine passion they focus on what that vision should be. It comes with spiffy words like *working smarter, not harder, ownership culture*, or *quality first* and is kicked off with multiple folksy get-togethers. It can come like a blizzard of Pareto charts and coloured belts with seemingly great science or authority attached to it across the entire business landscape, or it can be individualized like the many personality typing tools used in team building exercises. It almost always encompasses mandated training to modify and educate workers on the new acceptable behaviours that promote the desired new culture. Yet regardless of all this effort, expertise, and emotion, there is resistance to embracing and implementing these new teachings. At this point, if the leader feels they're to blame they will cycle through all the things again in the hopes that it's done better the second time. If the leader believes that their leadership team is at fault, then they will get new members for the leadership team and the cycle will be repeated. But if that leader's boss thinks they're at fault, then we get a new leader and the cycle starts all over again. This constant cycling of cultural mandates and leaders only deepens the cynicism of workers and builds a suspicion that the leadership doesn't know what they're talking about.

This cultural transformation failure is caused by some basic misconceptions that we have about business culture, revolutions, and the type of leadership needed to pull it off. The problem isn't with the various cultural concepts, cultural changing programs, or even the leaders and their execution of those concepts and programs. All is caused by some basic misconceptions about the mechanics of business culture and how to lead that change.

First is our concept of business culture, which isn't caused by people, but by people acting in a way proven to be successful given the set of circumstances. So, if you want to change the culture, you need to change the circumstances surrounding that culture – not the people or their behaviours.

Second is our concepts on leading change, which are all about value and how achievable that value is perceived to be. This is the foundation for leading change. Trust and adherence are the currency invested by followers in the rising and falling stocks of leaders. The more successful a follower perceives they can be, the more they're willing to invest. So how a leader manages that perception of success is more important than the actual change itself.

Third is credibility, as only capriciousness/reform can be promoted by the palace, only sedition/accommodation can be promoted by the nobility and only revolution/transformation can be promoted by the masses. Promoting the right type of change at the right level of the company goes a long way to determining the credibility of that change. Only by connecting between the three distinct classes of a company can you create the necessary resonating value, leadership, and credibility that sustains a change in direction, and makes it the new rule or order of business.

When the belief that failure was due to complacency, inability to adapt, and lack of accountability, it's worth restating that the real issue is a misunderstanding of the mechanics of culture and leadership. Leaders can warn of disorder and chaos and they can lead re-ordering efforts, they just can't be seen openly participating in disorder. Leaders for change have to leverage two sets of tools in order to be successful at change. One set for creating the space to change by managing a company's key asset, its people and their collective intellect. The other set is to manage orderly change or that gracious state of real fundamental change I call "Controlled Disobedience".

THE CHANGE ECONOMY

"Opportunity is missed by most people because it's dressed in overalls and looks like work." – Thomas Edison

In terms of corporate change in the 21st century we tend not to worry about which direction change should come from so it's legitimized, or if there's enough cultural space in the business environment to accommodate the desired changes, or even if we have the right conditions for acceptance to change. These are not common concepts, and yet understanding these concepts are critical for making and sustaining successful change. Through the next few pages, I will be explaining first the two motives for change, second making space and why it's important, and third, what are the three major indicators that determine acceptance, or what I call the "Change Economy".

THE TWO MOTIVES FOR CHANGE

In the typical corporate setting, there are basically only two reasons for change:

1. The Proverbial Gun

2. The Opportunistic Blur on the Horizon

The first reason is most fondly remembered because it has a very high success rate in promoting change– the crisis. That's when we're facing certain annihilation; the competition is going to eat us for lunch today, and we have everything to lose and nothing to lose all at the same time. When the proverbial gun is pointed at our heads and it's being held in someone else's hand, we tend to respond by dropping all the artificial barriers, everyone pulls together, and great things are accomplished in short order. It's those memories, experiences, tactics, and beliefs that we draw from when having to make change happen.

But 80% of the time the need to change is for another reason – for opportunity. This is when doom isn't impending, but a blur on the distant horizon, and its priority in relation to the present is arguable. On face value though, it's this type of change that's prudent to do, especially if you wish to be positioned to take advantage of the future and put your best foot forward now, instead of playing catch up later. Often it's in this type of environment that leaders with vision are trying to bring forward a case for change, and often they're caught trying to convert opportunity into crisis by bringing forward urgency and threat in the hopes of creating that fondly remembered sense of camaraderie and doing whatever it takes to get the job done.

When dealing with opportunity change, that sense of urgency is just not there and the need to fix that which isn't broken is not a compelling case for change. In fact, it's here that the mere direction of the message gets leaders or authority figures in trouble. In times of crisis it's expected or even demanded that the leader or leaders initiate change, that the enemy be identified, the boundaries by which to operate are set, and an inspirational speech given on the good virtue and qualities of those about to give it a good fight. In this time of crisis, a strong leader can be forgiven any suggestion for action, regardless of how wild or onerous it may be, because it's seen as trying anything to protect the organization or team.

In times of crisis it's preferred that those in authority are seen as authoritative and the best messaging is top down and directional.

In times of opportunity though, if a leader presses the case for change from the top down, to fix what is perceived as not broken, or worse, is perceived as wanting to break that which is working, then the credibility of that leader or leaders is eroded to such a point that the famous parable "The Emperor's new clothes" applies. People will smile and nod at the gibberish coming from management's mouth, but to their ears it all sounds like wanting to blow up the kingdom and stop doing the most successful things to everyone's ruin.

When a leader tries to blow up the very thing that gives them their power and authority, that will be likely seen as a formal abdication of that authority and it's at that point anything that leader or leaders have to say will be met with total disbelief and resistance either openly or passively.

(WHEN TO STOP) COMMUNICATING THE CHANGE

Of course, good leaders have been taught that the first step is to communicate the change, but when met with resistance it's often believed that the issue is one of misunderstanding or poor communication. So, they double their efforts to ensure the case for change is crystal clear, with a constant and progressive cycling of:

- Messages, slogans, and buzzwords all dressed up as the gospel

- Speaking at increasing levels of passion or volume

- Enhanced messaging with great wall art or posters and added as performance objectives tied to everyone's earnings

All these efforts are received as mad ravings or sheer lunacy that just create a higher degree of fear and cynicism with each recurring cycle to the point that the message is now seen as a blitzkrieg of arbitrary threat instead of a case for real opportunity.

Once the leader gives up and turns their attention elsewhere everyone breathes a sigh of relief and quickly return to their normal path.

This cycle will go on, repeatedly creating for leaders, the belief that people need to be pushed to change, and for people, the belief that leaders' priorities are as fickle as that "flavour of the month".

As this cycle repeats, every once in a while a happy accident occurs when the situation finally turns into a matter of crisis change and the lucky leader with impeccable timing will find that their approaches to managing change works wonders, everyone responds, rallies and pitches in to make the organization successful. That successful leader, now with great confidence, moves on to bigger and better things.

Of course, the cost for all that cycling that went on before is incalculably enormous and is the direct result of picking the wrong direction for making change happen. So, to package my long-winded words into one concise bite-size piece of knowledge, remember: when dealing with change for reasons of crisis, then a top down approach is best, and it's business as usual so do the things that come naturally. When dealing with opportunity change, it must be from the bottom up, and that requires a different approach. In this case leaders need to be aware that it stops being about making the case for change, and becomes about making the space for change.

THE COLLECTIVE CORPORATE INTELLECT

The third concept I wish to introduce, especially in the 21st century is that the real foundation that supports business is not people, process and systems, but something that's even beneath those basic things, something I like to call the "Collective Corporate Intellect".

If you ask most people "What is the foundation of a business?" the response after a great deal of synthesizing will invariably come down to people, process, and technology. But with a wry smile I would answer that it's the stuff contained inside those things. The foundation of any company is its intellectual capital, and what has not been questioned is just how much has the transition from the industrial revolution to the information revolution impacted our ability to maintain or enhance that capital using a previous era's approaches on leadership, organizational design, change, technology, compensation, and personal development.

Thanks to the industrial revolution, the division of labour, and mass production, we have come to take for granted that the foundation for every business is people, processes, and systems. It's through the management and interaction of those three things that tangible goods are produced. But do these mass production approaches designed for the tangible things we do, fully apply to things like immediacy, personalization, accessibility, authenticity, security, interpretation, and community? All are intangible things that create many of the valuable revenue streams that successful companies rely on in the 21st century. None of it is tangible in any form, and almost all of it's created by that collective intellect stored inside of people's heads, embedded in complex, parallel processes/relationships, and encoded as business rules in systems and knowledge stores.

This shift of the corporate bedrock has occurred in such tiny, microscopic steps over the last 60 years that we're totally unaware of this significant change, yet we feel the symptoms of that change each and every day. We've crossed over ever so slowly since approximately 1950, from the industrial revolution into the information revolution, and in order to excel in this new revolution we need our companies to formally recognize and start managing this critical asset.

We need to manage a company's intellectual equity and capital; in the same manner as we do our other forms of capital, be it human, financial, technology, or sweat equity.

Treating this intellect like an investment portfolio can allow us to shape that intellect to avoid pitfalls, sinkholes, and sand traps, or better target opportunity and advantage. If I'm planning to buy a lot of expensive technology but most of the knowledge needed to automate that function is inside people's heads, and if I leave it inside those heads, then my chances for success are not terribly high.

On the other hand, mapping out that intellectual capital and recognizing it's not invested properly means you can employ strategies to move that intellectual capital from one form into another that supports the process automation, or new behaviours required to support new products.

This cultural transformation failure is caused by some basic misconceptions that we have about business culture, revolutions, and the type of leadership needed to pull it off.

The first mistake is thinking that the foundation of a business culture is people and the way they think, when it's really the circumstances or space that governs what people know they need to do, to be successful.

Second, no credible leader can legitimately authorize the creation of disorder for that which they're responsible, which is exactly what change is, disorder for the purpose of re-ordering. That's why you never see any revolutions start in the palace. It always starts down in the streets with the unwashed masses that eventually work their way back to the palace.

It bears repeating again, leaders can warn of disorder and chaos, they can lead reordering efforts, they just can't be seen openly participating in disorder.

Leaders for change have to leverage two sets of tools in order to be successful at change. One set for creating the space to change and the other to manage orderly change or that gracious state of real fundamental change I call "Controlled Disobedience".

When you stop to think about how we go about justifying the risk and funding for transformation in corporations, it has an eerily similar feel to the modified Ponzi schemes that greased the cascading failure of the financial sector and the recent devastation of much of the world's economy. So, what's going to happen when the fiscal wiggle-room afforded by the fat in operational budgets and continued corporate growth all dry up? Will amortizing benefits far into the future be enough currency to invite risk and change in our companies? Is the level of mistrust, cynicism and disobedience that face most attempts at transforming the business, just the currency of a company's bankrupt internal change economy?

To survive in the 21st century business environment, competitive advantage will be gained by those companies that can manage risk and change like an investment portfolio, building a stronger foundation by tapping into the daily internal investment already taking place and dealing with that bankrupt corporate change economy in very tangible ways.

Survivors will be those that think of a company's intellectual capital as a tangible asset and begin to try and leverage that asset to the same degree or better than they tried with other critical corporate assets. Recognizing that 80% of a company's intellectual capital still lives in the heads of its employees, they must be treated as an investment in the company's future in order to gain access to that valuable capital. So as a first step, creating an operational team that manages your intellectual capital in very tangible ways leads to a deeper level of engagement that better prepares the business landscape for profitable change.

By actively working the change economy like engagement brokers, you grow both the employee and company investment portfolios to the point it radically alters the working culture, invites the future, increases opportunity, and decreases the costs often associated with attempting change or transformation.

THE ADMIRAL AND THE SAILOR: LESSONS FROM THE SEAS

There is a great analogy for how leaders when faced with change for opportunity's sake, make the mistake of not recognizing or accommodating the natural course or direction for this type of change, and how often the very change these leaders seek is often snuffed out by their lack of understanding, to the folly of all.

Returning home victorious after doing battle, an admiral was dogged by many days of bad, stormy weather. He could not beat the fog constantly hounding his fleet of five warships and approximately 2,000 troops every step of the way. Afraid that his fleet may founder on coastal rocks, the admiral summoned all his navigators aboard the flag ship for a conference to come up with their current position. At the end of this conference, the consensus opinion was that the fleet was safely west of the rocky shores of the peninsula.

Sometime after the conference, the admiral was approached by a crew member of his flag ship where the conference had taken place. This sailor, who claimed to have made a complete reckoning of the fleet's location during the whole cloudy passage, believed that the fleet was much farther north than the consensus gained at the conference by all the navigators. Unfortunately, policy was very clear that any navigation by an inferior was forbidden and considered a subversive act. This was something the seaman was probably well aware of, but considering the enormous danger everyone was in, by his calculations, it was worth the risk to make his concerns known to the officers. Of course, the admiral had the man hanged for mutiny on the spot.

As the fleet continued north, in short order they discovered to their horror that they had in fact misgauged their longitude and were really near those rocky shores they were trying to avoid. So, on that foggy night, that shore became the unmarked tomb stones for 1,400 sailors, as four of the five fleet warships sank to the bottom of the ocean. The flagship of the fleet hit the rocks first and sunk in minutes with all hands on deck. Only two men washed ashore alive, one of them being the admiral, giving him time to reflect on the previous 24 hours' events and what must have been the worst mistake in judgment of his naval career. As the admiral lay collapsed and spent on the sands of the shore, having hung the only man that could spit "I told you so" into his face, he was spared at least that humiliation, but unfortunately, a local women purportedly combing the beach found his near drowned body and the enormous emerald ring on his finger, and decided not to spare his life.

Following the right chain of command when it comes to change is the most common mistake made by companies trying to change.

When dealing with the immediate crisis, the chain of command is from the top down and has to be, in order to saves lives in military cases, and save profits or efficiency in a company's case. But in the case of change for opportunity's sake, the chain of command is reversed. I see it in meetings all the time; someone has a great idea and the boss rewards that person with the great idea by assigning them all the work or making them accountable for getting it done. The boss in front of everyone has just hung that poor sailor and made it a shining example of what happens to people who embark on subversive acts. Not surprisingly, the number of ideas that come up that are not the bosses are almost nil, and it's not surprising that the boss can usually be heard lamenting about the lack of creativity or ambition in their team.

Opportunity by its very nature is a subversive act and a tool to change the way things are.

As leaders it's not your role to come up with the ideas but to provide the extra capacity or space in the circumstances surrounding the opportunity, be it time, money, forbearance or resources.

INTELLECTUAL CAPITAL FRAMEWORK

Inspired by readings on knowledge and intellectual capital, there are three asset groups that come together to create what I consider intellectual capital.

1. **Data and information as an asset** – this is validated written or codified knowledge that documents how a company's policies, processes, products and tools are supposed to operate. This knowledge resides outside the minds of individuals and therefore is in an accessible state, with some hunting and pecking. It's in this area that a lot of corporate knowledge management strategies are focused and technology has been aggressively deployed. This capital is often measured by volume and usage, rooted in the past, it's the documented foundation for sharing validated knowledge. If a company or organization's intellectual capital is made of primarily this type of capital, then there is low agility and a high resistance to change. This capital is best suited for high volume, low cost/mature activities. This capital is highly susceptible to the information explosion.

2. **People as an asset** – this contains the experiences, attitudes, talents and knowledge of the individual. It's from here that our strategic visions for the future and leapfrogging innovative ideas germinate, then spring forth for benefit and opportunity. This capital is usually measured in terms of experience. Either experience with education in the form of diplomas, degrees, and certificates or experience with work in the form of responsibilities and job tenure. The hidden treasures of human capital are those unarticulated pearls of wisdom or tacit knowledge which can only be gained through experiential learning; this tacit knowledge is the foundation for generating new ideas or reclaiming lost corporate understanding. If a company or organization's intellectual capital is made of primarily this type of capital, then there is process fluidity, high resistance to change, with a bottom-up approach and not top-down driven change. This capital is best suited for low volume, highly customized/new activities. This capital is highly susceptible to the trend of decreasing job tenure.

3. **Relationships and context as an asset** – this most elusive and ethereal part of intellectual capital is called context. It's about the sound reasoning, which richer understanding of the relationships or circumstances that exist between third parties, information, knowledge, vendors, customers, marketplaces, organizations, people, and processes can bring. This capital is the launching pad for decisions, planning and action. It can reside inside the collaborating minds of individuals who are part of an organization, or may be partially codified in terms of contracts, service level agreements, and product specifications, and are measured in terms of number of relationships partners/networks/process/systems, and the speed of decision making. This capital is rooted in the present and is the foundation for knowledge integration and validation. If a company or organization's intellectual capital is made of primarily this type of capital, then there is flexibility, but not a quick rate of change. This capital is best suited for growth and complex optioning activities. This capital is highly susceptible to the accelerating complexity of technology.

THE KNOWLEDGE MANAGEMENT ENGINE

How knowledge is managed in the everyday work environment isn't really that much of a mystery. The knowledge management process is invoked a million times a day in every office, factory, or work site. This process may reside entirely inside one individual or be a collaborative venture performed by many people or businesses.

First there are businesses, organizations, and groups of people or individuals (people asset) who have an idea or thought. It can be a new idea to perform an old task or an old task performed at a different time, and so on. It's usually brought on by some small variation in the routine of the day. It's that imperceptible change to the working environment that kicks off the whole process of managing knowledge, which thanks to the human capital of a company is managed often seamlessly and without conscious thought.

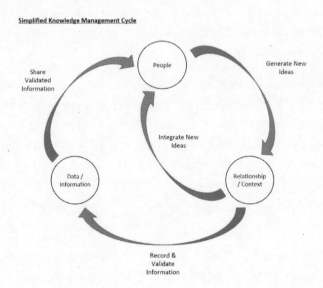

Nonetheless, the process starts with the generation of an idea to do something slightly different. This new idea is acted upon and integrated into the real working environment. This process of new idea integration involves making sound decisions or choices based upon an understanding of the current environment where the idea is to be integrated. Do I add my new idea after I complete this task first? Do I add this piece of information to it before sending it down the line and so on? That validating environment is an understanding of the relationships between third parties (relationship asset) like process, tools, systems, people, products and pricing. Integrating this small idea of change into the working environment immediately validates the effectiveness of that idea.

The results of this validation if considered of some value, is then recorded in a physical manner, committed to memory by the originator of the idea and then usually verbally to other people in the immediate area or community. If it's considered of great value, then the investment is made to write down these results and store it in a medium that allows others to share in this new understanding; usually in the form of bulletins, memos, or a reference in a central store. Depending upon the method and results of the validation, either people assets (by word of mouth) or data assets (by written word) have been increased. This new increase in intellectual capital can start the whole process over again because change has been introduced.

In a perfect world, this model is operating unabated and maintains a current relevant business model with very firm, level understanding and command brought on by the ever-increasing returns on the growing intellectual capital. This is the assumption made, that the business has a working knowledge management engine that's introducing new ideas, continually validating the way business is done and growing that intellectual capital, so it can leverage the latest and greatest technology has to offer.

The reality is this engine is often broken either internally by well-meaning policies or processes that impinge the ability of people or organizations to integrate new ideas, share and record new understanding or by those external factors, technology complexity, job tenure, and the information explosion. This broken knowledge management engine creates an uneven and infirm landscape for knowledge, reasoning, and understanding. This intellectual landscape can resemble towering mountains of impervious rock with an unwillingness to change or blowing shifting sands that makes it hard to figure out which way is up. It's in these types of business terrain that we try to build our mega transformation projects at very great expense.

As the foundation for intellectual capital is attacked, a company's ability to reason is seriously incapacitated. This leads to those common symptoms of incomplete requirements, inability to envision new concepts, lack of understanding of value and lack of focus or commitment which plague business and drive failure. Taking a closer look at how the accelerating complexity of technology, decreasing job tenure, and shortened business and technology life cycles are attacking the foundation of a company's intellectual capital, and encapsulates the root reasons that are driving the failure of our IT/business transformation projects. The business can't know its business because it's forgetting more than it's learning and therefore can't have expertise over its business domain. If you don't know who you are and what you should be doing, then you can't know what to change.

Allow me to share another story to illustrate this point. Let's say you have a 2x4 framing stud with a nail sticking halfway out. Your home renovation project is stalled because you can't lay that next piece of wood down, with that nail sticking out. You look for your hammer and start driving that nail in further. But the nail isn't going in easy. You need a bigger hammer. When it still does not go in, you get a sledgehammer, and finally after some delay, additional costs, and a lot of sweat, that nail is driven flat into the stud. You continue on your merry way. This is the typical approach used in companies to solve their business problems. But 99% of the time there was a simpler and more subtle answer to the problem.

So, think of a business problem, just like a nail and a hammer. You have a nail sticking halfway out of a piece of wood. You need that nail flush with the wood so you can lay the next piece of project down on that wood. The hammering you're doing isn't getting the job done. The obvious answer is to get a bigger hammer or a bigger hammerer!

When that doesn't work, then a brain storming session is called to look for out-of-the-box solutions. The suggestions are wild and fanciful, "use a 1,000-pound wrecking ball", "weld two metal plates on each end of a metal pole", "lay the plate against the nail and drive a truck into the other end of the pole". A consultant is hired to review the suggestions and then they offer their innovative solutions. They will tell us people elsewhere use nail guns to drive nails into wood. We could modify the nail gun so it can drive in already partially nailed nails.

After great expense and delay, the new pile driving nail gun is rolled out to finish the job, along with the required air compressor and extension cord. Except that solution only worked in that specific case. In fact, it works for 40% of the time, while most of time there is no electricity to run a compressor, which leads to new rounds of brainstorming and innovation on portable power or portable compressors.

Now what if during this entire exercise there was someone sitting in the background, someone from the frontline, who is dealing with this problem every day. Except every time they spoke, they talked about clearing a path. Everyone would respectfully pause with perplexed gazes, listen politely and then go back to talking about how to drive a nail; the frontline person would eventually understand their place was to watch and keep quiet.

The problem is the language spoken by the frontline person. They couldn't frame their understanding in a way for others to see. The solution isn't driving in the nail but merely pulling it out. For that you can use the claw side of the hammer, or for tough jobs, different length crowbars. Simple, cheap, and quick, and in the end it achieves the same thing, a smooth surface on which the next plank can be laid.

So often our business problems can be solved by merely understanding how we work today. It's all about effectively using the intellectual capital existing in your company. This process is simple, easy and quick.

BRIDGES PRINCIPLE 3: PREPARING THE SITE FOR CHANGE

PREMATURE TRANSFORMATION

Our final story is also the most often told. It's an example of a self-inflicted chronic performance anxiety disorder called "Premature Transformation". It's where corporate desires get ahead of corporate reality. It almost always starts out as a three year, $100 million, great big transformation project, and usually ends as a tale about a technology death march. A death march that's only brought to conclusion when a company can't spend any more money because the price tag is getting too big to hide and the story to the shareholder isn't going to be a nice one to tell. So, when something, anything, gets implemented, the project gets promptly killed with the appropriate story attached about changing priorities or aligning with market realities.

At the ensuing recognition bash, you will hear the stories about how the technology people were pissed off with the business because they had to work around-the-clock to take the latest in technology, dumb it down, and in the end produced what amounts to the basic capability of a spreadsheet. The business was pissed off with the technology people because they were delivered a spreadsheet (and a crappy one at that), when all the business wanted was a calculator. Finally, the finance people were pissed off because it meant countless late nights as they tried to maintain some semblance of integrity and what few friends they had left, as they simultaneously figured out a way to ethically hide the wasted money and rip money out of people's budgets, for benefits not delivered.

I just used two hundred and fifty words to describe something that occurs approximately 4,500 times a year in companies all around this world and is caused not by bad technology, poor design methodologies, lack of project management or even missing engagement, user involvement, or executive sponsorship, but by not addressing the level of understanding that the business has prior to defining the vision, identifying the problems and designing the solutions for those best laid plans. You can't see what you can't understand and people in companies understand less now than at any other point in the history of modern companies. The one question never taken into account before starting a major exercise in change is – are we at the right level of thinking required to contemplate, let alone support this change?

BUILDING THE BRIDGE FOR TECHNOLOGY CHANGE

REALIZING THERE ARE NO EXPERTS

The use of computer technology in a business setting is relatively new when compared to other disciplines in our civilization and culture. In 1946, the first programmable computer, ENIAC was created, and it was the first computer that could be tailored for use by any enterprising company. That is, if that company had the funds and floor space available to afford dealing with a computer that contained over 17,000 vacuum tubes and 7,200 crystal diodes. The computing power of that beast hardly compares to the sleek rack-mounted servers that number in the hundreds, even thousands sitting inside a typical large company today of say 20,000 or more employees.

Yes, technology has come very far, very fast. So fast in fact, that almost all technology has passed by the needs, convenience, and therefore the comprehension of most people living on this planet. You can include me in that group, and I consider myself as someone who is tech-savvy. Remember how many VCR's would continually flash 12:00 because the average person couldn't figure out how to program the clock, even with exhaustive documentation. Of course, VCRs and DVDs are now obsolete, internet streaming and media centers having taken over. Advancing technology has stepped in to solve the flashing clock issue by auto-synching their time to the internet or cable source. We don't even have to know what time-zone we belong in.

If you look at the simplest of technologies sitting in our households, we are utilizing barely 50% of the total functionality, be it our coffee makers, toasters, or microwave ovens. As a matter of fact, I would like you to grab your microwave oven user guide, count the total number of features it has, subtract the number of features you actually use and what you have left is what I call your "TDF – Technology Dissonance Factor". On average, a microwave oven has 10 functions related to cooking and the timing of cooking, and 10 functions related to setup. We use six, maybe eight out of the 20 functions offered. That's a 60% TDF. You're utilizing 40% of the total capability purchased in that microwave oven. But I know when it comes to microwave ovens, we measure value based upon things we're expecting that microwave-oven to do well; cook our meals fast and evenly. This technology is simplistic and cheap, so we don't really care that we're only using 40% of the total capability.

Now, transfer this concept to a major company wanting to transform its business using the newest, most complex of technology available. What percentage of the issues, delay, and the $120 million cost is related to what the business really needs? Almost all if it's related to the TDF – that 60% you don't use.

An acquaintance of mine, a budding professional project manager once told me that "The customer is the expert on what they want, and it's up to me to translate those wants into tangible actions to be delivered." He promptly went on to deliver a work flow system that eliminated 50% of the automation the customer previously enjoyed and also added two new manual functions that needed to be staffed, all in an effort to satisfy the number one customer requirement, 100% visibility of their work and all for the low, low price of $10 million and two years of effort.

In the resulting post mortem it was determined that the majority of the time and expense was spent in trying to get the non-conforming data from the old legacy systems into the new workflow system in order to satisfy the number one customer requirement of 100% visibility of work. The resulting two new manual functions were necessary to deal with missing non-conforming work that could not be put into the system. The 50% degradation of automation was a conscious decision taken to satisfy the number one objective. Given all the options, the customer really wanted to maintain the current automation capability and gain 100% visibility of the work that they could not see at that time, which by the way was all conforming data and therefore very easy to implement into the new workflow engine. The customer did not need to have all work into one system, although that would have been nice.

Everyone called this a communication issue and lack of clearly articulated requirements. But that's merely the symptom. The real culprit was lack of visualization by both parties and not knowing what isn't known. What was the impact to the business if it had two workflow systems? Was value still gained? What if we break existing capability, will the new capability be more valuable? How hard is it to make non-conforming things conforming? What is non-conforming and conforming data? All are questions that usually can be answered after the fact.

Because of this Technology Dissonance Factor, the customer can never be the expert and articulate accurately what they want from technology, because they can't even begin to visualize what that technology can do and how it may alter their business.

Now add to this mix another new reality that every business is losing or forgetting the very rules and reasons for why they do the things they do in their business processes and procedures. On average each year, a business operation can expect to see 25% of their core business change either with policy, products, personnel, competitors, pricing and on and on. That amount of change means that the business operation would need to be devoting a portion of their organization to do nothing more than assessing the changes and resulting impacts to their business, if they were aware of the changes and those impacts.

A lot of times the business is too busy doing its business to know what is going on in its business. These internal and external change factors are impacting most companies with a host of Corporate Alzheimer's-like symptoms resembling memory loss, confusion, and lapses in good judgment. Suffice it to say that the business's lack of comprehension of technology and its difficulty in remaining current with its own business, makes it impossible for the "customer to be an expert on what they want", which are only those things they truly need to succeed.

In the IT world, the high priests and priestesses of business technology are not impervious to both the Technology Dissonance Factor and Corporate Alzheimer's. In fact, it's even worse for those poor souls who have chosen a career guiding technology for benefit. Computer software and hardware is advancing at an incredible rate. It's impossible to be absolutely current on every new breakthrough. Because of this proliferation of products, upgrades, and version releases, it's career suicide for any IT person to devote themselves to one technology, one product, and become the supreme expert on that product and its impact on the business setting. That's a sure ticket to obsolescence. So, while technology gets more complex, IT specialists are forced to become technology generalists, or as the old saying goes, "jack of all trades and a master of none".

If we look back at days when "Big Blue" IBM mainframes were in their prime in the '60s and '70s technology and its relationship with business appeared to work well. On the business side you had a high degree of business function expertise and low degree of business change with a long strategic planning and product life cycles. On the technology side we saw a limited number of technology products with a long product life cycle, so this enabled a high degree of expertise on any given product and its capability in business terms, plus time to learn of any new capabilities and their implications to form and function. It's from this era that a lot of our corporate governance, readiness, change management, design, development, and planning methodologies were developed, refined, and codified into what are now our traditional approaches for managing technology and its change in the world today.

In the end, it really doesn't matter if you're a proponent of the waterfall method, agile methodologies, extreme programming, spiral model or Win-Win spiral models and so on, because they'll rely on one important and critical foundation which is sadly missing – the business must be able to see and know exactly what it needs and that's no longer a reality.

Over the last 15 years or so, a number of studies have been conducted on why IT projects fail. In the end they all came up with a similar list of key factors such as:

1. Limited user involvement

2. Weak executive management support

3. Unclear statement of requirements

4. Poor planning

5. Unrealistic expectations

6. Unskilled and inexperienced staff

7. Diluted ownership

8. Lack of clear vision & objectives

Other than Item 4 which can be any number of duly documented Planning Guidelines or Rules, and Item 5 which is just a risk mitigation strategy to "only risk small things", the other six items' success factors are all relative or subjective terms whose foundation is dependent upon confident, competent, engaged, and passionate people or groups of people.

So, we can forget about technology, methodologies, and project management. The key to success are people who are experts and know what they're doing. Yet, I just spent several hundred words saying that there are no experts anymore. Wars and terrorists aside, Donald Rumsfeld may have been on to something when he said 'There are known knowns; there are things we know we know. And we also know there are known unknowns, that's to say, we know there are some things we don't know. But there are also unknown unknowns – things we don't know that we don't know."

UNDERSTANDING PREMATURE TRANSFORMATION

The concept of using computer technology for business gain and transformation is barely 60 years old, which by civilization standards is something still in its infancy. Given that people are the foundation of successful IT transformation and can't hope to be expert enough to know the "unknown unknowns", then is there another area, another industry that's older, that has faced similar issues and come up with a successful way to deal with this problem? A way of making "known knowns" out of "unknown unknowns"? When I started searching, the answer was a quick and surprising yes.

There's another industry that has architects, engineers, developers, contractors, designers and project managers. In addition, it also has at least several hundred years of history, lots of learning through experience and real live successes that have stood the test of time. The similarities between the business/IT/computer software industry and civil engineering and construction industries are so aligned that they could almost be considered parallel universes. Both industries have to deal with dynamic environments, new technology, governmental, and environmental concerns.

If you start to think of software code, applications, and packaged systems as logical superstructures rising high above the varied and uneven business terrain which consists of many different business processes, cultures and objectives, then logic would seem to dictate that by understanding how construction projects deal with the "unknown unknowns" may lead to some solutions or new approaches for the business/IT world to try.

The big question is how you equate business cultures, people, processes and IT technology to dirt, rock, weather, concrete, steel girders, bulldozers and dynamite. But before I go into greater detail in subsequent pages, let's first start by comparing the basic approaches between construction mega projects that build skyscrapers, bridges, or pipelines, and business/IT mega projects to see if there are any significant differences in approach.

MY JOURNEY – THE REALITY OF CREATING SUSTAINABLE TRANSFORMATION

I won't lie to you, when I was a frontline manager, I thought for sure the problem with getting systems implemented were caused by totally incompetent people in IT and the business support areas. When you're an operations manager, you're continually asked to spit blood, grind employees, and limit capability in your team, all in the name of making budget reductions of 10% or more each year. Well, it all becomes so very disheartening watching as these mega system projects blow millions of dollars trying to figure out things like project roles and responsibilities which are perceived as wasting the equivalent of 20 years' worth of frontline blood, sweat and tears for no tangible benefit or gain. This all leads to that thriving experiential cynicism – the survivors – that's the trademark of so many frontline business cultures. So, it was from this place that I embarked on my journey to solve the chronic problem of bridging the gap between the complexities of technologies and getting some sort of business benefit in a timely and cost-effective manner.

STEP 1: WE THOUGHT IT WAS OBVIOUS…

The first step in any problem-solving journey is always towards the obvious. I thought the solution to our problems was nothing more than simply hiring some bright and eager people with some software developing skills and letting them loose in the business to do good things. Initially that's exactly what happened, and we saw instant success with some very simplistic applications which served a starving market. But with successes come growth and more complex problems requiring more complex technology. Soon I was starting to see all the same typical problems or disconnects when implementing technology for business benefit. You know those well chronicled symptoms; misunderstandings of business requirements, communication breakdowns, loss of sponsorship and attention, cycling of key subject matter experts, missing delivery dates, and finally wholly inadequate and unyielding solutions to the current problems.

SUCCESS BREEDS CHALLENGE...

We started to hit the same walls that all "skunkworks teams" have hit over the last 20 years. You know, rogue or barnacle applications that are flaky and one of a kind, poor documentation, spotty support, adding complexity to business processes and in some extreme cases even risk to the health of existing mission critical legacy systems and applications. All the things that don't make fans of this type of strategy, especially the IT and the process improvement folks in a company.

So, there I was at that obvious first step, my little "skunkworks team" doing great things and encountering all the same problems that everyone else had encountered before. It was another manager, a peer of mine, who introduced me to an old saying when I was giving him my tale of woe. The saying hit me like a lightning bolt. *"The significant problems we have can't be solved at the same level of thinking with which we created them"* – *Albert Einstein*

My first assumption that incompetence was the root of our chronic failures was wrong. I had successfully proven that I and the people who followed me were just as incompetent. Needless to say, operating under that first assumption made my working relationships with the business improvement and IT folks adversarial at best, and downright nasty at worst. With Albert Einstein's words clanging around in my head and a little egg on my face, I started to look at this problem from another angle.

STEP 2: UNDERSTANDING WHY PREPARATION
FOR TRANSFORMATION MATTERS...

The second step in any problem-solving journey is almost as obvious as the first. If it's not incompetence, then it must be the way we use technology. Armed with this new thought, we started to explore how approaches in leveraging technology impact change and the environment around us.

The impact of skunkworks or rapid development puts simplistic capability in the hands of the frontline business, and this becomes compelling and even intoxicating. The value resonates immediately with all levels of a company, from the senior executive to frontline team members. The instant gratification of this approach is addictive and that's why companies continually gravitate back towards skunkworks or "focused" solutions. So often these initial successes seduce us into trying to expand focused solutions to take on bigger and bigger issues, or worse, we think that with the shotgun approach, we can "skunkwork" our way out of our problems, which inevitably leads to a disconnected patchwork that ends with disastrous results. We know using drugs in isolation or as the complete cure can often be destructive, mask the root issues, and lead to bigger problems

On the other hand, enterprise IT technology is meant to be used as an end state strategic solution, designed, planned, and engineered. It's meant to be the technological foundation for the whole company and must deal with all aspects of that enterprise. Legacy system transformation projects are the equivalent of open-heart surgery, or even more dramatic, heart transplants. We know that surgery requires a lot of organization, planning, infrastructure, and expertise to successfully pull it off. It can't be rushed and done haphazardly.

There exists in many large companies this constant and unhealthy push-pull conflict between two polarized and diametrically opposed positions, the need to just get it done quickly and the requirement to do it right the first time. This constant pendulum swing back and forth is driven by changing corporate priorities with respect to short, mid, and long-term needs. The resulting horror stories from zealously adopting one approach over another, prevent companies from maintaining a balanced program which would allow the leveraging of both strategies for mutual benefit.

So in keeping with this new train of thought revolving around drugs, patients and heart transplants, if skunkworks technology is going to be used as a drug, it must be used as a means to an end, a managed path, and not the end state or solution itself. Then focused or skunk works technology, like drugs, stop being destructive and become essential, vital and necessary in the patient preparation prior to surgery. Let us take this analogy a little further, a patient is diagnosed with a heart problem and requires radical surgery, like a heart transplant. The surgery is the end state solution or cure. Prior to the operation, weeks or even months in advance, the patient is put on a structured regimen in preparation for that surgery. This regimen will often include many types of drugs. Drugs to lower cholesterol, thin blood, balance the secretion of hormones or chemicals, and so on. These drugs are not directly part of the solution. They are, however, the critical preparation path to the solution. After the surgery, a new regimen may be prescribed, but this will be in support of the new heart, or "the end state solution".

LEARNING FROM FAILURE...

IT transformation projects in companies are just like heart transplants. Massive changes to the very core of how that business needs to function and operate. Yet the current practice is to spend a great deal of time on requirements gathering and scope setting, all devoted to designing the future modes of operation, the new processes and the new technology needed for the cure, the end state solution, and determining the type of surgery to be performed. Business readiness activities are devoted to understanding the degree of change to the business and readying the business for its new tasks and functions after the transplant has completed post-operative healing. Then of course there is the actual transplant surgery which include all the activities and tasks required to perform the transformation. But what project activities are devoted to preparing the patient (or in this case the business operations) for that surgery? Who's devoted to ensuring that the heart will be accepted and not rejected? Who's responsible to ensure that business operation has stable vital signs and the right frame of mind to survive the operation?

Armed with this new concept of patient preparation, I changed the entire direction and focus of my little team. The objective of focused solutions or skunkworks is change itself. Through technology we can use change in stages, to prepare business cultures for the coming transformation.

As luck would have it, a great opportunity to test this new train of thought came our way. You remember in the previous chapter I talked about that project manager acquaintance who lead the charge to deliver a $10 million workflow application that cut business automation by 50% and increased operating costs. Well I stepped forward and proclaimed that our Quick Win Collaboration team could build a replacement for that workflow application for 5% of the original cost and in one quarter of the original time spent to deliver it. All bold promises that later looked like they were going to become the death of this little team and a testament to my arrogance.

With change as our focus, we tried to do all the right things. We had user forums every step of the way, focus groups, top subject matter experts fully engaged and giving all their work secrets. Our team was embedded day-to-day in the actual frontline operations. We had executive sponsorship and attention. We even had the full support of the IT group, even though there was much to risk for them if our team succeeded at what it was trying to do. We designed a workflow and work management application built specifically to promote scheduling flexibility and enabled rapid change from the business. We staged rapid iterative releases of capability all designed to manage change for the purpose of enlightening the user community. Yet we were failing miserably, money all spent, two months past the delivery date, no users, no confidence, no workflow, and no business benefit.

On a subject matter expert review call with all the business areas involved, we were going over a final list of some 87 critical action items, the last issues that needed to be cleared up before the business was ready to consider using this application. The majority of these action items were conflicting with each other. We had seven distinct groups which had 3 different business and process models. All the business units were very passionate about the need to maintain their business models.

At that point, we knew if we continued to do the same things over, our list would just grow from 87 to 887 and we would be nowhere closer to achieving our goal. Some business teams were ready to go and salivating at implementing the application, other groups were close but needed just a couple of tweaks and other groups were a long way from even considering moving on to this application. Yet all them were fully engaged and primed for changed. **We had succeeded at creating a sustaining environment for change. But it wasn't working when it came to managing change with different groups or cultures**, all competing for or conflicting with each other because of the different needs or agendas.

To succeed we needed to deal with the business environment in a totally different way. Not as known patients with a set, prescribed program that fits the needs more for the coming surgery, but a way that accounts for and manages many differences and large scale variations; this can then offer insight and understanding on what's required to create a strong bridge between the needs of today and the strategic advantages for survival tomorrow.

STEP 3: FINDING THE PATH TO TRANSFORMATION SUCCESS

The third step in this problem-solving journey came about in an unusual way. I live in a growing suburb of Vancouver, British Columbia, Canada. There used to be nothing but open fields, trees and untouched mountains in my area. Over the last 15 years, a lot has changed. There has been an explosion of residential, retail, and industrial development in the area. Every day I drive, walk or cycle by no less than fifteen or sixteen major construction sites in various states of readiness or completion. It was in this environment that I found myself wrestling with that impending workflow project catastrophe, when an epiphany of the obvious occurred.

There I was standing in front of three very large mounds of dirt piled to different heights and levelled off on top. I remember it was a little more than a year ago that I saw lots of dump trucks and bulldozers dropping and moving that dirt around and then nothing for months. The only thing that gave away the intentions for that land was a billboard advertising three retail big-box outlet stores and their impending occupation of the land.

Now it seemed that things had started up again with trucks, bulldozers and surveyors. They had to prepare the land first before they even thought about building any type of structure. Each one of the three piles of dirt were there to pre-load the land. Each had been designed to the custom specifications needed to support each building in the project and deal with the different terrains and soils that lay underneath those buildings. That's when a new framework for looking at business, technology and change for business benefit started to come together right before my eyes and that framework is the basis of this book.

While the drug, patient, surgery analogy was great for helping understand the benefits of technology from a focused solutions versus "end state solutions" perspective, it wasn't applicable when trying to understand how to manage purposeful change when dealing with multiple business cultures, agendas, and objectives. However, looking at the business environment like the terrain of the earth and how we deal with land preparation for the purpose of building does.

Looking at the business environment in this way, immediately you could see why we were experiencing spotty results with our workflow experiment. The groups that were ready to jump onto the tool all had process and business models that called for a high degree of optioning when dealing with groups of work and customers. Their business terrain had a degree of form and stability but was malleable like clay or compacted dirt. The groups that required more tweaks on our workflow tool were very hard, stoic business cultures that dealt with high volume and regimented work. They mimicked all the characteristics of hard granite rock. The last groups that were nowhere near ready to use the workflow application all had very fluid processes and business cultures. They all dealt with highly customized work with specific customers and mimicked the characteristics of sand.

The flaw in our tactics wasn't in using technology for the purpose of change but trying to use one approach with technology to manage all aspects of that purposeful change.

Two months after splitting that workflow project into three distinct and targeted solutions, like customized levelled mounds of dirt used to pre-load the land, we had implemented workflow in all areas with great benefit. At the time of this writing, one group has migrated to our new IT transformational end state solution and the other two groups have since consolidated into a next generation workflow solution which we built for them. All this done as a preparation step before they move into new IT transformational end state solution sometime later in the coming year.

While we took a few wrong turns to get here, when you stop to think about it, it all makes perfect sense. The foundation of any IT project is critical, and the common assumption is that all IT projects will be built on level land that can support the weight and load of the solution. Yet when you look at a lot of the big IT project failures, the solutions were fine, it was the fact that their foundation was built on very uneven and unprepared land (business cultures).

BRIDGES, OIL WELLS AND SKYSCRAPERS — TRANSFORMATIVE CHANGE IN A COMPANY ISN'T THAT DIFFERENT...

What I realized through my own journey,was that there was more to learn when we explore other well-traveled paths. As a civilization we have been constructing big earth-shattering structures for thousands of years and the practice of civil engineering has been around at least since the beginning of the pyramids. Along the way there have been many failures and more will come as we continue to stretch beyond our current limits by building higher skyscrapers, longer bridges, and deeper oil wells. There is a long and rich history of construction mega projects which have tried, tested, and honed those processes for planning, designing, and building the engineering wonders of the world that are now commonplace in our civilization.

When comparing the very young computer/IT industry with the very old civil engineering/construction industry the cast of characters is eerily similar. Both have architects, engineers, contractors, designers, developers, project managers, analysts, technicians, certified trades people, and customers who start out with nothing more than a picture in their mind. It stands to reason that similarities would exist as both industries are rooted in engineering.

Civil engineering is at the root of the construction industry and it has been evolving as an applied science over the last 200 years with specificity and deeper understanding for all facets that impact the design, growth and advancement of the world's infrastructure. Today, there's an ever-growing list of disciplines that come under the civil engineering banner; construction, environmental, geotechnical, hydro-technical, material, structural and transportation engineering to name but a few.

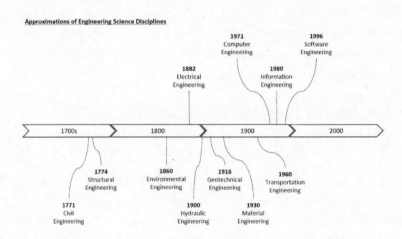

Approximations of Engineering Science Disciplines

On the computer/IT side we're just starting to see a burgeoning growth in the universities as an applied science. But really with the first computer science degrees only being handed out some time in the early '70s, computer science is still in the very early stages of development. So much so, there are still debates about whether there is such a thing, as software engineering. Computer technology and how it's impacted by the world is mostly an uncharted and unexplored landscape. 100 years from now I'm sure we'll see similar advancements and understanding of the environments and their characteristics that impact computer technology as it's deployed for benefit in the world; it will provide command over the environment similar to what civil engineering disciplines offer today with their understanding of things like the tensile strengths of materials, the elasticity of soils, and the mechanics of fluids.

PROCESS OVERVIEWS – "UPON FURTHER REVIEW"

When I started to take a look at how both IT and the construction industry go about building mega structures, it appeared to be totally different worlds, with different terminology and different challenges. But the more I read and the more I started to peel back the onion, the more a high-level comparison model started to take shape. At a very high level both processes are identical. Every project has an initiate, design and finally a build phase.

When looking at the initiate phase the mechanisms, strategies, and techniques for scoping and requirements gathering are identical. Only the cast of characters is different.

Experience and knowledge about the specific and unique industries play a big part in the quality and accuracy of forecasted timelines and estimated budgets. But I'm sure statistical techniques and models are probably very similar.

When looking at the design phase, similarities can be drawn between the two industries. In the construction world, architects take the learning from those strategic scoping and customer requirement sessions to come up with an overall ascetic view of the finished structure, be it bridge, building or tunnel. Usually this is represented back to the customer in the form of a rendered drawing of the finished product. In the IT world that rendered drawing of the overall view is usually in the form of a systems road map.

The next stage of the construction design process continues to take this two-dimensional drawing and add structural depth, weight, and form to it. Designing the right mixture of material and bracing to be used requires an understanding of the impact space, function, and stresses potentially have on these structures. Again, in the IT world, the structural or operational view is enhanced with a better understanding of the mission critical core business functions, mapping of the processes and a better understanding of relationships between key stakeholder groups and their systems. The construction design evolves further in detail by adding building services like electricity, elevators, water, and air flow. In the IT world, this design stage is called the systems view and it enriches the design details by adding a better understanding of the subroutine or task/functional interaction between applications and systems.

Finally, in the construction world, with a fleshed out, detailed design, a better understanding of the load and geotechnical impacts this structure will have on the surrounding environment is gained and appropriate measures are taken to prepare the surrounding land to support the project. In the IT world, at this stage a technical view looks at the fundamentals of technology from protocols and data structures to processor load tolerances and system latency.

The build phase for the construction process is pretty straight forward; start at the bottom and work your way up. Place the foundation, then the structure, walls, floors, ceilings and finally the roof. Next is the plumbing, electricity, windows, doors, and floors and carpets. Finally, it's the cosmetic touches, landscaping, ornaments, signs, plus any minor issues like sticky doors and ripped carpet.

In the IT world, it starts with the pre-alpha version of the software, the foundational design and schema. Next in the alpha phase, the logical structures are built including the data schema, business logic or rules and then the presentation layer. At the "beta" phase of the build the logical structures are reinforced with added functionality and capability. Finally, the software is released and if it was done right, then at this stage, it's mostly minor bug fixes. When comparing at a high-level, processes between the two industries appear very similar.

But if you were to conduct a poll of business executives and were to ask them which returns more value for the dollar, construction or software mega projects? The answer would be very lopsided. A company can spend $300 million trying to transform technology to enhance their billing capabilities and get nowhere. But for the same money you can get an eight-lane bridge that spans a large river, or a 40-story skyscraper that houses thousands of people. As I stated earlier, we have been building physical things for a very long time, our experiences are richer and our sciences more evolved, so it stands to reason that we would be better at construction mega projects.

To my mind, the pinnacle difference between both industries, the fundamental reason for successful delivery on construction projects is a parallel process that's not readily acknowledged as part of the formal process but is implemented on every single construction project throughout the world. This parallel process is often rolled under other titles from preconstruction activities to site certification and logistics. It starts, sometimes prior to the first architectural drawings, can act like a conduit of information throughout the design process and typically doesn't end until the building foundations have been laid. When looking at this parallel collection of activities in isolation, it's commonly called site preparation.

SITE PREPARATION – COMPARING CONSTRUCTION AND IT TRANSFORMATION PROGRAMS...

In the construction world site preparation can occur just about any time it needs to; from the moment a person or company purchases land, even though they may not know want they want to do. It can start right after the first architectural drawings or just before the construction crews show up. There is only one hard and fast rule, sites need to be prepared prior to the first brick being mortared, lump of concrete poured, or pipe laid.

The activities involved in site preparation range from clearing debris, land excavation, grading, trenching, soil compaction and stabilization all the way to building drainage systems, access roads and erosion control. If the site isn't prepared in the first hand, then a lot of money is wasted on material, machines, and people expending great effort trying to get into and working around the construction site. But a more important role played by activities involved in preparing the site for building is bridging the gap between the assumptions made by architects and engineers for the purpose of design and the realities of what is needed to complete the actual physical work, in other words it's a proactive and critical reality check.

The moment that first bit of topsoil is turned over, it can uncover a myriad of "unknown unknowns", bring deeper understanding and significantly alter designs, budgets, and timelines for great savings, very early in projects. The activities going on during site preparation are significant and need to be done in coordination with architects, engineers, and project managers. This is done to ensure that the preparation enhances, not hinders the project and is also necessary to ensure free flow of information and learning between site preparation outcomes and the requirements of the design. Below is a sample of some significant site preparation activities. In this case it's $10 million worth of preparation for a $300 million power generation plant.

- Clearing and grubbing approximately 90 acres

- 75,000 cubic yards of topsoil stripping

- 64 acres of soil stabilization

- 196,000 cubic yards of excavation

- 172,800 cubic yards of structural fill

- 63,000 tons of stone base material

- Storm-water drainage, including 30 catch basins,

- 4,000 linear feet of concrete pipe culverts

- 600 linear feet concrete pipe

- 4,500 linear feet of access road

- 20 acres of seeding

- 60,000 yards of erosion control matting

Early in history, real life experiences taught people involved with the building of bigger, better, taller, and longer structures that it requires both an understanding in very specific terms the ground on which we build, along with the structure being built, in order to significantly increase the probability of success. The earliest and most famous example of this is back in 1138 when Italian builders reached the 4th cornice of the bell tower they were building in the town of Pisa and the whole thing started to lean. Over the next 190 years through great feats of engineering and construction, that tower rocked back and forth on unstable land until completion of the 9th floor. It's now an infamous oddity and testament to the determination of humanity.

In a lot of ways that leaning tower is a great metaphor for challenged IT mega projects that so many companies have been experiencing over the last 20 years, but without the tourist revenue generating opportunities enjoyed by the town of Pisa. Understanding the mechanics of soil and the art of preparing land for mega projects has been a great enabler in leveraging technology for the building of the world's infrastructure and it's a concept that's almost entirely missing in the evolving science of computers and our current business processes for leveraging this technology for benefit.

In this new era of the information economy, the foundation of any company is not their people, processes, cultures and decision-making chains of command, but the information, knowledge and wisdom that resides in those very places. How a company manages and prepares that foundation of knowledge determines the success, failure and value to be leveraged from their investment on computer technology.

The term site preparation becomes a very tangible, practical, and critical activity when focused on a company's working knowledge capital. These activities can produce all the same properties and benefits that civil engineers, architects, and construction projects reap when levelling, excavating and pre-loading the very land their projects will stand on.

BUILDING THE BRIDGE: GETTING PEOPLE ON YOUR SIDE

BUILDING THE BRIDGE FOR CULTURAL CHANGE

Our three stories, Shuffling the Deck Chairs, Flavour of the Month, and Premature Transformation, are amongst the worst ways to prepare for change, and yet companies do this time and again without thinking that the corporate intellect is a tangible thing, just like people, process, and technology needs to be considered and managed as the first step in preparing for opportunity and change. These stories teach us that to greatly enhance your chances of successfully transforming culture, gaining competitive advantage and creating tangible business benefit in the new normal, you need to consider three important things.

First, business value no longer comes from a company's people, process and technology nor its products and services, but instead comes from the smarts that reside inside of those things. Similar to oxygen, when companies begin labouring through change without first tapping deeply into their intellectual capital, they tend to find sound business reasoning in short supply. To compensate for this, businesses desperately inhale whatever resembles intelligence and the resulting hyperventilation leads to that chronic level of oxygen-starved decision making commonly found in most corporate mega-projects.

Next, 90% of a company's intellectual capital resides inside the heads of its employees. But thanks to globalization, ubiquitous connectivity, and declining long-term employment, a company is no longer filled with a captive audience of dutifully obedient workers willing to relinquish this valuable asset. Instead, these employees are more likely to resemble very mobile, savvy investors looking for a place that gives them the best return on their sweat equity gained from leveraging that intellectual capital. Just as in the stock market, where investor confidence determines whether it's a bear or bull market, in today's business environment, successful transformation rests on the level of confidence these internal investors have in the changes for the future. If they can't see it or feel it, then they take quick flight, sometimes in body but usually in spirit, and along with it an unhealthy portion of intellectual capital and the ability to gain profitable benefit from it.

Lastly the insight necessary to drive innovation, change and transformation is no longer a requirement that can be gathered on the surface of a business environment. Buried by the unrelenting realities of a 21st century business world, insight must now be excavated with purpose and intent, otherwise you end up muddling along trying to do what is considered the right thing to do, instead of gaining advantage from having done what was the smart thing to do.

Significant results will happen when you take into account the new normal and close the gap between strategic intentions and tangible benefits by bolstering confidence, excavating insight, and managing in very tangible ways the most valuable asset a company has, the intellectual capital languishing inside its employees, processes, and technology.

The construction industry understands well from the lessons of life that you prepare the land first, if you wish to successfully build for benefit and profit. Looking at the evolution and proliferation of the various sub-disciplines under civil engineering, you can surmise that not only is it important to understand the technology of engineering in order to continue advancement and innovation, but equally critical is wisdom and knowledge about the impact the surrounding environment has on that technology.

This is a hard lesson we're just starting to learn in the world of using computer technology for business benefit. The use of traditional tools for mapping, documentation, and training in preparing the business for the new technology is key, but companies must expand into a burgeoning area, not yet fully evolved called site preparation, in order to change the current success rate that IT and business have when implementing technological transformation. Site preparation, with its focus on the environment about to be changed, is the missing link to preventing our companies from not leveraging technology fully and wasting millions of dollars on something much less than a spectacular result.

When preparing land for construction, it's one thing to call in bulldozers to move dirt or use dynamite to blast rock, but it's a completely different thing when dealing with the corporate intangibles like communities and cultures which are at the best of times complex, and at the worst, chaotic. But, what if the characteristics of our planet's complex environmental processes which govern our weather, the air we breathe, and the land we walk on, can also be applied to the relationships that exist in companies when using people and process for purpose and profit. It stands to reason, if this is true, then we should be able to take some basic concepts that govern complex relationships in the outside world to help understand better the dynamics and complexities going on inside our companies. Looking at the corporate environment like rocks, dirt, seasons and weather can offer us new insight on planning and preparing the corporate landscape for human-made change.

NICE ANALOGY, SO YOU'RE COMPARING PEOPLE AND BUSINESS TO DIRT

This is where I need you to invest in the next few pages before you immediately condemn me to the local psychiatric ward. In the game of innovation, today's preposterous thoughts are tomorrow's great ideas. Unless of course, it was just a stupid idea, then mercifully it's forgotten quickly. In order to bring some semblance of order to the inner workings of a company and create sustaining value, action, and change, while mitigating the extra fun stuff of intrigue, hidden agendas, and politics, you must look at the corporate world as having three distinct layers:

1. **The Executive Branch** – Vice Presidents, CIOs, CFOs, CEO, Board of Directors

2. **Middle Management** – Directors, General Managers, any other of the thousands of imaginative titles that are used in this layer. Also included are business support people like business analysts, and performance leaders

3. **Frontline Operations** – Any person directly involved with the core functions of the company including the Supervisor or Immediate Team manager.

Now if you compare these layers with the three basic components that make the outside world go round, the atmosphere, the land and the laws of nature, you can begin to explain the internal forces at work in a company and even begin to predict or forecast the change of seasons and the type of weather about to be experienced. Taken even further, you can begin to see challenges and plan accordingly when dealing with different terrain in variable weather conditions during different seasons of the corporate year. Too often we think of the corporate environment as a series of very complex Machiavellian situations that are as unique as the individuals involved. This way of thinking only invites a career of getting blindsided by wild, unforeseen variations and being at the mercy of unseen forces, much like our ancestors, the early Homo sapiens who often resorted to lucky charms, sacrifices, and paralyzing trepidation when witnessing change.

In fact, the corporate environment is a deterministic engine which creates patterns and cycles which over many years of experiential learning become the foundation of practical wisdom found in many corporate veterans. Good decision making comes from the wisdom of that developed sixth sense, that intuitive pattern matching that leads to the "spider senses" tingling, déjà vu, or that feeling you can't put your finger on when things don't add up. Understanding the mechanics of the corporate environment in terms of air, land, and laws of nature, accelerates the ability to make sound decisions, and plan and manage the situations around you.

You're probably wondering why water isn't part of the basic components given it's so critical to the proper operation of any environment. In the context of a company, I think of water as money, whether as wages, expenses, revenue or profit, and I feel that the impact of money inside companies is probably the most understood of all elements and does not require further explanation at this moment in time.

THREE COMPONENTS OF ANY COMPANY – THE AIR, THE LAND, AND THE LAWS OF NATURE

You know the old corporate axiom for bosses, "The higher you go, the thinner the air, the $%#%'er bosses get". You can go ahead and fill in the blank, as I wish to remain gainfully employed. But the basis of all humour is partially rooted in a fundamental truth, and the partial truth here is, there are distinguishable layers that exist in a company, and the bosses are always at the top. Air is essential for life and it's our corporate executives that maintain that atmosphere for benefit and purpose.

Good executives have the ability to operate in rarefied air. They must be able to operate with minimal information, be able to fill in the blanks, draw conclusions and in the interest of global concern, always look far in advance of the current position. That's why we associate ideas like "the big picture" and "50,000-foot view" to the executives of a company. That's why their actions must not be perceived as being localized or regional. They're responsible for the global well-being of the company.

Down at ground level we don't give the atmosphere much thought. You can't really see it. You breathe it, but that's a reflex action done without thought. It's only when is it missing or in short supply that the impact is felt and then, when you can't breathe, immediate and debilitating panic sets in. The size, substance, and beauty of the earth's atmosphere can only truly be appreciated from space. That's why executives value external recognition or marketplace distinction.

Unfortunately, that's also why at the frontline or ground level good executives are not acknowledged for the value they bring, and bad ones create panic and kill the Earth. In the pursuit of action, executives who go exploring at ground level find everything to be heavy, slow, and the simplest things appear to require great energy. To the global-minded/ blank-filling executive, at ground level there is an explosion of minutia, a dense atmosphere of information. When meeting with the frontline folks, executives experience blank filling overload as they try to understand the far-reaching ramifications of the thousands of details that have been presented. This overload is usually followed by the blank, glassy-eyed stares of these executives who are coping with what is for all intents of purpose, deafening noise; unfortunately, the ground level people don't get the hoped-for response or action because of that overload.

Conversely when frontline people have great need and wish to bring their concerns up to the executive, this often requires climbing the highest land masses, and they find thinking in such thin air very laboured and slow. It takes great effort to talk and think in the simplest terms. To the unencumbered executive, a sense of concern and wonder overcomes them as they watch ground level people operate in their high-altitude environment, giving the appearance of being frail; plodding Mount Everest climbers requiring an awful lot of equipment like rope, oxygen bottles, pickaxes and pitons, all in order to survive the typical executive environment. This gives grave concern to the average executive about the state and health of the ground level environment, as the atmosphere is critical to the survival of a company and this is the exclusive domain of the executives.

There's danger in using urgency and fear to gain the attention of an executive. This feeds into a nimble executive's desire to act quickly and create sweeping global change, which is often done using the direct approach, moving great masses of atmosphere, which is another way of saying generating a lot of nasty hurricane-force winds that blow in those changes. But if your concerns were less than global in nature, then you've been very successful in generating a lot of collateral damage, and believe you me, your colleagues are taking down numbers and remembering names.

Of course, fear of widespread damage could create the "Emperor's New Clothes Syndrome" where nothing but good news is presented to this layer and nothing of consequence can be achieved. When handling proper change in this environment I often think of an old Aesop's fable.

> *"The Sun and Wind were arguing about which of them was strongest. They decided to hold a contest to see which one of them could succeed at getting a man walking below to take off his coat. The wind blew and blew directly on the man and his coat. The harder the wind blew the more resolute and determined became the man's grip on his coat. There were six villages, five farms and a complete forest decimated by the wind. The Sun then came out and warmed the air. Soon the man unbuttoned his coat, and shortly after, when the air was hot, off came the man's coat."*

Now on one level the moral of this fable is supposed to be that you get more with gentleness than by force or you get more with sugar than vinegar. On another level, I see the moral to that story as "you can't mandate change from the top". The man and his coat are a metaphor for change. The value of the coat is it keeps the man warm. The more the wind blows, the colder it gets, the more valuable the coat becomes. Executives trying to mandate change just entrench resistance to change and people hunker down in their foxholes, tighten the straps on their helmets, and ride out the storm. We need executive change to be focused, not on the change itself, but on those aspects of the corporate culture that retain the value in resisting change and gradually devaluing that resistance.

As an example, you can get the executive to tell people they better change or else they'll lose their jobs. Some people immediately go find work elsewhere, some people work twice as hard at what they do to prove the error in that decision, and others, usually the majority, decide to take their chances and hunker down and ride out the storm because if it's as bad as you predict, then you'll probably be gone long before they will. Instead, in gradual steps you introduce the external threat that's driving the need for change, and then detail the counter measures along with the resulting potential success. Next, demonstrate a cultural focus on re-use, reinvestment, and employee value. Then recognize and reward those who take the plunge.

Change is a bottoms up activity; the executive layer can't directly create it. I still believe that no revolution ever started in the palace; it has always been in the streets. The big secret is almost all revolutions were secretly supported by royalty and the privileged helping create the climate for change.

We understand the complexity of roles and perspective in every organization and in order to build a successful change program, we need to understand how to bridge multiple drivers and enablers of change.

CONNECTING THE BRIDGES: THE PLAN

MAKING IT HAPPEN

So for me, the Bridges Principles of Knowing, Managing Knowledge as an Asset and Site Preparation, need to be applied with the important understanding of the universal tenant that *the business is too busy doing its business, to know its business, so we have to help the business gain new understanding about the things it needs to succeed at its business.*

What do all these words mean? To use technology to teach and educate first, and the rest will follow. If the business is using pen and paper in their daily operations, show them the virtues of using a spreadsheet. Don't change their process; just open their eyes to that next level of opportunity. If the business has four different processes for delivering a service and the end state goal is to automate, then support each existing process, heighten the strengths and weaknesses of each process. This leads to better understanding and new ideas which lead to collapsing processes and gaining obvious automations. Use technology as a way to prepare the business for change and not just assuming it's the end result of the change itself.

This book could be viewed as the equivalent of a lay person observing an apple falling from a tree and pondering what forces and framework might be at play. I was fortunate to have the opportunity to test this framework out over the past five years in a real working business environment. A saying comes to mind when searching for a way to adequately describe the tangible results created by following this framework.

It came from a colleague, Farzaan Kassam, who engineered the growth of this experiment into an enterprise-wide program. He spoke these words at a recognition event involving some 60 or 70 people out on a client's office floor, to honour the positive impact this program had on a rather large business unit of several hundred people responsible for the delivery of telecommunication services. Farzaan said, "The impact of change is hard to discern, sitting in an office or meeting room. The proof is always in the pudding and the pudding is always out on the floor." I'm convinced that this framework or hypothesis I'm about to describe has merit, and has been refined while using it out on the floor in real business environments, watching it grow and prosper, achieving yearly significant tangible benefit, and finally seeing that experiment turn into an enterprise program whose foundation continues to adhere to the truths of this hypothesis.

THE MAKING OF A GREAT PUDDING

I was given an exceptional opportunity that spanned over seven years starting in 2000 to create, implement and mold an experimental organization devoted to understanding why change in business is so difficult and what can be done differently about it. I was able to bring in some of the brightest young minds that our universities had to offer on technology and business. I was given almost unfettered access to the business operations to experiment and prove that transforming culture, gaining competitive advantage and creating tangible benefit through change can be made quickly, cheaply and almost painlessly.

When I left in pursuit of writing this book, I had witnessed how two people focusing on a small obscure service process, can grow into over 100 people working with an entire enterprise of some 30,000+ employees and delivering in excess of $100 million in accumulative benefit, while reengineering over 47 corporate processes, providing significant competitive advantage and gaining international recognition. The cost over the entire seven-year period was less than $20 million, meaning that for every $1 spent paving the way for change in this way, the company had gained $5 in net new tangible benefit. Proving that by taking a structured approach to connecting to the intangible side of the business environment, you can engage your business to a deeper level that will reinforce the foundation for change; through understanding and insight, this will lead to a higher degree of competency and innovation needed for change along with active acceptance and sponsorship to sustain change.

I ran this organization devoted to change, and all these concepts described in this book were honed as I worked with these bright young minds and molded them into business coaches for change. They had to work directly with the business, negotiate the right to change, use technology as a teaching tool for change, and deliver tangible, verifiable benefit from that change. This experiment confirmed that change can be a simple and cost-effective process when made an everyday journey with specially trained guides that ensure business practices the act of changing. Through this practice, you can sustain your existing business while building a solid foundation for change by gaining deeper understanding and insight on what should be changed, a higher degree of acceptance and sponsorship to change and the competency and innovation needed for change; all things a company needs to survive in the 21st century business environment.

ANATOMY OF THE QUICK WIN COLLABORATION TEAM

The Quick Win Collaboration Team came together over a period of several years, but through that time the foundation and principles built and refined through blood, sweat, and tears proved to be a robust and sustainable change engine for any organization. The team was centered around a core belief that *"as technology continues its relentless march as a commodity, embedded into all aspects of our everyday life, the more our thoughts, ideas, and actions, in collaboration with the communities around us, become the real differentiators in competitive advantage and customer value."*

This belief stands the test of time and reminds us that it's the *knowing* and not the *knowledge* that makes the difference in successful change.

We were intentional in our naming. "Quick Win Collaboration" said it all and meant that our focus was on quick change, meaning that change would be in bite size pieces that the organization could absorb and find tangible value. We defined collaboration as *the interaction among individuals and communities that can encompass a variety of actions, such as communication, information sharing, coordination, cooperation, problem solving, and negotiation.* There were no heroes or mavericks in this process. Everyone understood that it was the individual insight and ideas coming together that created the magic in the solution.

Our mandate was "*To be accountable for supporting the strategic and tactical action plans of the leadership team and their operational units*". In doing that, our Quick Win Collaboration Team dedicated itself to becoming a recognized industry-leading support organization by making everything accomplished real and measurable, maturing our skills in managing knowledge as an asset, and integrating Quick Win collaboration philosophy into enterprise change enablement fabric.

The foundation of a strong community and team were based on three distinct components including a non-negotiable set of guiding principles, a firm belief that an extended team of shared services, knowledge, and new talent was an essential ingredient, and a disciplined approach to continually engaging all levels in the organization throughout the program.

QUICK WIN GUIDING PRINCIPLES

1. **The frontline user is always our starting point** – Frontline teams are closest to the core business in any organization. Overall, front line management has the slowest rate of churn, therefore the largest body of knowledge. Frontline is the most scarred and jaded of groups due to technology failure brought on by the knowledge gap. This provides the most efficient opportunity for cultural success.

2. **Immediate business value – the value proposition behind our method of engagement** – It's how we get people to partner with us on a journey of learning. That value has to be in the same timeframe of the community we're impacting, the frontline, which is near present. That means value must be felt in two days, two weeks, or two months. Anything else is outside the frame of relevance to the frontline operations. Benefit must be articulated into three perspectives:

   • Frontlines – Intangible Benefit *(e.g. getting rid of 50% of the unnecessary phone calls)*

   • Middle Management – Tangible Benefit *(e.g. reducing costs by 10 %, or deferring growth until next year)*

   • Executive – Good Will *(e.g. improving cycle time on key strategic products)*

3. **The journey of learning is more important than the design of technology** – The Quick Win value proposition is in new understanding or reclaimed knowledge previously lost, which leads to new opportunity and benefit. Technology is merely a means to an end in this proposition. It's the structured journey of exploration, experimentation, and education that breeds success. Quick Win Collaboration is about closing a knowledge gap and not a technology gap.

4. **Decisions are always made with balance and leadership** – These simple yet foundational principles are part of onboarding and daily coaching for the core and extended team, and reflect the team mindset and leadership culture.

   • When you make decisions that only benefit you or your team, you're being self-serving and acting like a **victim.**

   • When you make decisions that only benefit the business unit, you're being short sighted and acting like a **hero.**

- When you make decisions that only benefit the company, you're being pious and acting like a **martyr.**

- When you make decisions that benefit all three, you're being balanced and acting like a **leader.**

5. **We partner with the frontline, we manage ourselves, we guide the leadership, and we share with the executive** – We create a partnership of trust and action with the frontline. It's through managing ourselves and ensuring we live to our principles of Quick Win that creates this foundation or consistency of integrity that drives a cyclical partnership of engagement by way of common experience and trust in guiding the business leadership with new found knowledge. Because of the breadth of experience gained and credibility, we can share with the executive's critical points of interest in helping to create a new found understanding on the business issues at hand.

6. **Mistakes of commission are to be supported and recognized** – Measured risk and action are key components of innovation. People need to be supported when striving for results. Results fuel our engagement model and lead to greater benefit and learning than mitigating risk and therefore a learning opportunity for all.

7. **Mistakes of omission are not to be tolerated** – Not engaging front line people for the purpose of further understanding; not putting up your hand and asking for help when failing; not understanding the business value of your actions; these are all behaviours of omission that go against the core values of Quick Win and can't be condoned or sanctioned in anyway.

THE RIGHT TEAM

The Quick Win Collaboration Team actively modelled the guiding principles and the team was organized to focus on delivering on its mandate. Several unique roles are critical to consistent delivery of the

Quick Win principles. The roles focus on Value Synchronization, use of Appropriate Technology, Knowledge Management and Integration of all Quick Win initiatives.

Value articulation is the fuel for the collaborative action engine that gains attention and garners support needed to implement action and deliver results. This in turn generates brand new value to start the whole process over again. A **Value Synchronization lead** is responsible for:

- Understanding the relative value of all new initiatives, active or deferred, in our Quick Win Collaboration Team;

- Ensuring line sight of this value from the frontline team members up to Senior Leadership and Executive through benefits review sessions with all Quick Win team members, regular meetings with Directors, and adherence to the benefit sign-off process;

- Interlocking with enterprise corporate initiatives to ensure linkage and context of value is maintained;

- Providing hands-on support for the acquiring, accessing and managing of all funding and governance for initiatives; and

- Confirmation and formal reporting of benefits delivered and negotiated reinvestment of that benefit.

A key success factor is ensuring technology is leveraged for maximum effect by understanding which capabilities of technology are most appropriate to the environment and culture intended to be supported. Low cost and low maintenance with a high degree of flexibility are requirements of prime importance. Intentionally coined the **'Appropriate Technology' lead**, this role is responsible for:

- Managing the sustainability and growth of the Quick Win Collaboration Team hardware Infrastructure including Purchasing, Project Management and Support of all hardware and operating systems in play;

- Guiding resource on the tools and approaches of technology used by Quick Win – investigation and experimentation of new software innovations or trials in the context of business environment;

- Communicating and facilitating discussion on Technology strategy for Quick Win and building of Quick Win technology roadmap; and

- Leading the introduction of new technology concepts, approaches, and innovations – Collaboration with architecture, system development & support organizations to ensure line of sight of current priorities

A key priority is to continually enhance and evolve the philosophy and skill set of the Quick Win Collaboration Team through Knowledge Management and implementation of processes for the capture and retrieval of relevant information ensuring proper alignment with our existing business environments. The **Knowledge Management lead** is responsible for:

- Implementation of a sustainable measurement of organizational agility;

- Implementation of innovative approaches to knowledge management; and

- Capturing and recording the results and benefits of Quick Win initiatives and the cultural impact on the organization.

It's also important to foster the development of the next generation Quick Win Collaboration team by expanding and reinforcing the positive qualities of the Quick Win approach across the enterprise with collaborative links into IT, HR, Finance and Business Process organizations. The **Quick Win Integration lead** is responsible for:

- Provide integration consistency across hiring practices, integration sessions, and counselling on assignments;

- Develop guiding principles with umbrella framework that align all Quick Win activities including a governance model for all teams to operate under; and

- Support collaboration activities including quarterly vision sessions with extended teams across the collaboration community and maintaining Quick Win methodology and documentation.

I've packaged up these lessons learned through years of trial and more errors than even I would care to admit. These concepts to be told won't be easily believed, as they're right angles to common convention, and they often weren't when I shared them with the new recruits of our program. Only after they got smacked on the side of the head by failure and experienced the carnage and mayhem of promoting change for the sake of opportunity, would my words begin to resonant and gain a ring of truth and credibility.

Even years later, alumni from this team who have since fanned into various businesses around the world, continue to prove out how much they have come to rely on those early lessons learned on why the misconceptions about ourselves, organizational culture, and leadership in times of change, lead to the mishaps, missteps, and mistakes that so often plague our attempts and how best to avoid them by preparing the business for opportunity before you begin the journey of change.

The roles of this team were critical to enabling sustainable transformation and I'm pleased to share some reflections from Andrew Ah Yong, one of my early collaborators and partners.

> *As an alumni of the Quick Win team, I often reflect on the experience from that time and find that I am also often still leveraging those principles and approaches. Twenty years ago, I was an energetic and eager new grad looking for a fun and challenging job to build up my resume. Never would I have thought that as an inexperienced developer, I would be part of something transformational so early on in my career. I was wrong... but didn't realize that until much later on.*

The Quick Win Collaboration Team started as a small group of similar individuals who loved technology and were not burdened with "real world" processes or experiences. We were malleable in our ways since we didn't have the baggage or scars from traditional IT. What we lacked though as individuals was the sherpa to guide us on our journey. Someone who navigated the chaos and ambiguity of corporate culture, who wasn't worried about protecting his own career, but was focused on doing what was right for the team and for the business. That's where Richard Bridges came in. Our humble guide that had taken us on this journey of discovery and transformational change.

"The business is too busy doing its business to understand its business."

This was Bridges' Law #1 that he repeatedly reminded us. At the time it seemed obvious. We were sent to the end users, sat down with them, and tried to learn and understand their jobs. From there, we would identify opportunities, brainstorm with them, even teach them how to use their computers and internet differently. We would take those learnings and build applications for them, making their lives easier and letting them focus on the more challenging part of their jobs. Talking with end users, understanding their perspectives (and sometimes hearing them complain about their "management") and giving them solutions just made sense. What wasn't obvious at the ground level was we were helping them not just better understand their business, but we were helping them understand the potential of what technology could bring to make their lives better. We were there to design and evolve the technology with the end user, not build a solution that the end user wasn't ready for.

This may seem obvious at first glance, but what I've found during my experiences working within the IT industry is that there are natural and organic constraints that develop which counters the approach. For one, interacting with the end user rarely happens. Most businesses have enablement teams that often represent them, removing the distractions of projects so they can focus on their jobs. Although they have best intentions, they are often so busy with enabling, they are steps removed from the day to day business, losing sight of the actual operations and what these end users have to do to make processes and technology work. Second, it's also rare that the developer would be the one engaging, that's the role of business system analysts (BSA). Similar to the enablement teams, the BSAs are scaled to be efficient with working with the enablement teams, putting them steps away from the actual technology and development.

The key problem we have is the layers that are naturally created between the end user of the product and the end users creating it. Waterfall is a great example of how we have well defined steps and roles to IT delivery in order to bring clarity, structure, order and ultimately predictability in delivery. The issue however is the business is never static and is now changing at a faster pace than a traditional waterfall delivery cycle, making whatever was asked for likely out of date by the time development even begins.

As the IT industry realized the growing problem and paradigm shift, another series of methodologies came along – agile. Through scrum, kanban, SAFe, and other similar agile approaches, we have overcome the latency between requirements to delivery, bringing value to the end users faster and more relevant. Unfortunately though, it does not fully close the perception gap between the developers, BSAs and product owners. Agile methodologies definitely help resolve issues and understandings faster through the iterations, but success will still be constrained when there are multiple layers between the end users and the developer. It can be argued that stand-ups and scrums solve this problem, but in the end, if it wasn't the end user or the developer that wrote the user story, you've started playing the Telephone Game.

In overcoming the challenges, one of the key components of the Quick Win team was within its hiring approach. In order to purposely avoid the multiple hand-offs naturally existing in these processes, the team focused on hiring individuals with a combination of strong business acumen as well as technical understanding. They were individuals that could roll up their sleeves, sit with the business and understand their day-to-day, then build solutions that could make their lives better. Another key aspect that made this unique was the principle that capabilities had to be delivered quickly, so the end user could see the results and start the journey with us. Any solution built had to be delivered within 2 days, 2 weeks, or 2 months to create and maintain the velocity and engagement.

Transformation in the form of a guided evolution

A key outcome of the Quick Win principles is the grassroots engagement model it fosters – the tradeoff is the ability to scale. The challenge is that if not coordinated, multiple teams can be formed, each successful, but none can fully realize the potential of the ability for change they can drive. Inflection point between being short sighted incremental improvements to large scale transformation is the point where the culmination of multiple 'quick wins' can be orchestrated so they drive to a common outcome. As articulated earlier in this book, there are multiple steps leading to a building being built (the transformation) – each step being purposeful and preparatory for the next. Coordinated leadership and technical vision/ oversight is what differentiates the model from being a grassroots skunkworks organization to a successful transformation enabling team.

It's the culture, not the process.

Transformation isn't a one-time event, and it never should be. Successful companies and individuals are constantly having to change to stay relevant in this fast-paced world and the ability to foresee the need is just as important as the ability to initiate, lead and embrace it. A common practice is to bring in the fresh set of eyes or industry experts – but rarely does it work if they aren't empowered to make changes or learn on their own; quite often the new blood is brought in and implicitly forced to conform. To create the culture for transformation, you need to foster and cultivate the disruptors, they are the voice and champions of change.

It's easy to look back at the days when the Quick Win Collaboration team was formed and in its prime driving business and IT changes across the organization, and attribute it to different factors or variables. The model can be mimicked and modified, but success won't be guaranteed unless it's authentic and properly invested and supported. What is key however, is understanding and fostering the culture Quick Win guiding principles create. In the end, it's this mind shift and tuition that we have taken with us and continue to leverage that make us successful. Ultimately that's the real legacy and desired outcome of this approach.

THE FINAL QUESTION

There is a very important question that we as business leaders fail to ask ourselves before embarking on a journey of change or transformation. **Do I want change, or do I want improvement?**

It's because we don't stop to understand the difference between these two words and their important relationship that directly leads to the less than spectacular results achieved after spending so much, time, effort, and money on our strategically important transformational projects.

This confusion which ultimately leads to poor performance or even worse, project failure, stems from believing that change, improvement, and transformation is either one in the same thing (the business generalist's point of view) or mutually exclusive (the business expert's point of view). Perhaps an oxymoron but they're simultaneously, one in the same and mutually exclusive.

Improvement is all about timing; faster, shorter, tempo, frequency, and cadence. Change is about direction; a shift. You can have improvement without change, which is improvement purely from timing. You can have change without improvement, which is change that never lasts. You can have change with improvement or vice versa improvement with change. But like charged particles with the same polarity, they tend to repel each other and fail to bond, making the change and the improvement fleeting and unsustainable. Transformation is when you create a field that maintains the bond between change and improvement.

As I shared earlier, I'm not your typical business type person that would write a book. I have no PhD's, MBA's, or any other accredited degree or diploma. I've spent 90% of my thirty-year career in the telecommunications industry and mostly with one company. I never got past middle management. I've been called both the greatest thing since sliced bread, and possibly the worst manager on the face of the earth. I don't like to bow or show undue reverence to authority, I like to use humour in my dealings with people and situations, and I display absolutely poor timing when using that humour.

All of these acts may seem like horrible afflictions in terms of the typical business environment and fashioning a successful career, yet these afflictions compel me to question all that I see, not to take myself so seriously as to limit my thinking and to get into all sorts of messes that smart people with any sense would avoid.

As a result, I've been afforded many opportunities to gain different perspectives on change, be it from the bottom-up, the top-down or in the middle getting killed by both sides. This has given me a unique insight into the unfiltered workings of change at all levels of business from the boardroom, to the bathroom, and all the way down into the boiler room.

Now my irreverence, humour, and bad timing should have gotten me fired long ago, but instead merely limited my climb up the corporate ladder. This lack of career gave me the freedom to look at what was best for a given circumstance and act without regard for the personal or political well-being. It was because of all this that I was given an exceptional opportunity to create and mold an experimental organization devoted to understanding why change in business is so difficult and what can be done differently about it.

So, while I do use humour throughout this book, by no means does that mean that what has been written is a joke. These are real things I'm revealing, real things that will help you, real things gained from my experience with the inner workings of corporate life and from conducting this seven-year experiment on change which is still ongoing. I just choose to use humour as a way to dispense these truths, which you now know is both my strength and my affliction.

This book has been about preparing for and dealing with uncertain change in business. Change when the big boss or bosses want it, but everyone else isn't quite sure. Change when the company is doing great, the pay cheque is fairly certain, and threats are small dots in the murky far distance. This isn't change in the face of crisis, but the opportunity to change to get ahead of the game. It's almost never absolutely critical, just prudent to do. It's the smart play if you want to avoid crisis down the road or the smart play if you want to get ahead of the competition. But it's not going to put bread on the table today.

This is the type of change that faces most business, most of the time. It's the hardest type of change to initiate and accomplish because it's open to distraction, compromise, or both. These opportunities for the future which are usually things that keep leaders up at night or by day fretting about the lack of progress and the need to act now; these opportunities must compete with the business's pressing priorities of that day and usually it's no contest. Recalling again one of my favourite quotes from Edison, "*Opportunity is missed by most people because it's dressed in overalls and looks like work.*" It's not surprising what people in companies traversing this process optimized, digitally connected, be smarter business world of today are not looking for, is more work.

In addition, thanks to technology and globalization, those challenges sitting in the far-off murky distance have the ability to kick in warp drive, travel faster than the speed of light, and overtake your business. This is a real dilemma that's forcing companies to stop treating change as a separate episodic event from their business. It's very similar to the transformation that professional sport has gone through. In the old days and regardless of the sport, there was the season, the off-season, and training camp. Training camp was used to prepare and get in shape for the season.

Today, professional athletes have a year-round regimen to maintain fitness and manage fatigue, there is no off-season or training camp.

Coaches and their staff barely have enough time to assemble and assign, let alone alter personnel and plays, before they're into the business at hand of winning and losing. The 21st century business environment has become the same, but our approaches to living with and managing change have not.

So I hope through the course of this book you have been introduced to why people in companies are impeded from seeing, embracing, and taking advantage of change, how to go about dealing with change that's not top of mind, but maybe should be, and positioning the future as a structured every-day event so the foundation for change is readied, and your business can take advantage of opportunity.

ABOUT THE AUTHOR

If you looked in my dictionary for the definition of a corporate revolutionary, you would see Rick Bridges' name. Synonyms for a revolutionary
include rebellious, renegade, factious, insubordinate, rabble-rousing,
inflammatory and agitational. Rick would have proudly stood by those
descriptions of himself with a chuckle and quick retort about how thin
the air gets in those corporate ivory towers. But when you needed to
create data driven transformation, he was the best man to call. Rick
would lay out the plain and simple facts of your business, and more often,
than not, he would share the truths that may have been in front of you all
along but perhaps obfuscated by noise or complacency. Although some
were not ready, or perhaps were unwilling to hear the naked truths about
their organization, Rick never relented to politics or self-preservation. He
was always authentic, genuine, and honest about what was needed for the
business, or more importantly, its people.

Like all of us, Rick aspired for recognition but on his own terms. He
did not want the confines of a fancy title and his greatest moments of
satisfaction were when executives he worked with would pause and he
could see the light bulb go on in their heads. As you have read through
these chapters, what shines through is his passion and belief for building
change from the ground up, and embracing the history and insights
within your organization, as you build the future.

Rick and I were always very different in style and approach, but I learned
more from him than any other colleague in my career. We had a unique
partnership, he the rebel; and me, the annoying voice of reason. Together,

we built teams that shaped strategy and drove change from the ground up. It was always tumultuous but also the most rewarding and fun times in my career.

Over the years, my family had the great fortune to become close with his fabulous wife, Cheryl, and devoted daughter, Kelsey. They were his strength, and although Rick accomplished many things in his career, his family was always his greatest source of pride.

Rick was a maverick, a man ahead of his time, a man generous to a fault, and perhaps his only downfall was sometimes his truth hit too close to home, and the corporate world found his pill too hard to swallow. The world lost Rick in January 2019 after a courageous battle with cancer. For all of us who knew and loved him; he shared with all of us, the mind of a genius, the heart of a lion, the quickest wit, and dedication and loyalty for all who worked under his wing.

Rick's final hope was that he might share his life's work dedicated to connecting business to deep seated transformation. He had wanted his mother, Lois, to know his dream of writing this book would come true. I'm very grateful to Cheryl and Kelsey for letting me be part of this journey to bring his work to the world and to you.

In my final conversations with Rick before his passing, I was reminded of Winston Churchill's quote, "We make a living by what we get, we make a life by what we give". Rick gave us all several lifetimes of strategic insight, mentorship and of course, his friendship. Many have been blessed by his generosity. Many thanks to Andrew and Peggy Ah Yong, Farzaan Kassam and Erin Pankratz for the collaborative efforts to bring these chapters together. It has given us all a little more time to remember and enjoy stories and memories of our dear friend and mentor.

In reading this book, we hope you will have taken away a few nuggets of insight and appreciation for a story that we can all apply as we seek to improve our own journeys as we make our mark in the world of transformation.

Joanne Campbell

Printed in Canada